SCUBA DIVING IN MAJORCA
THE 50 BEST DIVES

JUAN POYATOS
ANÍBAL ALONSO

SCUBA DIVING IN MAJORCA

THE 50 BEST DIVES

EDITORIAL MOLL
MAJORCA
1998

Collaborators:

Material, equipment and boats: Isurus, Tritón
Control and management: Aina Gelabert
Photographs: Carlos Huerta, Jaume Serra, Toni Torrens, Aníbal Alonso and Marc Chicano
First correction: Catalina Torrens Font
Collaboration: Pilar Languil Ripoll
Edition and design: Susanna Moll
Aerial plans: Conselleria d'Obres Públiques
Aerial photographs: Banco de Santander
Cartography: Servicio Geográfico del Ejército
Graphs: Juan Poyatos
Medical adviser: Federico Sbert
Biology advisers: Maria Valls, Miguel del Pozo, Ana María Abril

First edition in Spanish: December 1996
Edition in English: May 1998
Translated by: Elizabeth Lynch-Cummins

I.S.B.N.: 84-273-0796-9
Legal deposit: B-31.365-98

Printed by BIGSA
Manuel Fernández Márquez, s/n
08930 Sant Adrià del Besòs - Barcelona

CONTENTS

INDEX OF DIVES
classified by increasing difficulty
AND THEIR LOCATION
(Maps from the Servicio Geográfico del Ejército
Cartografía Militar de España, Serie "L")

_____

* No boat needed

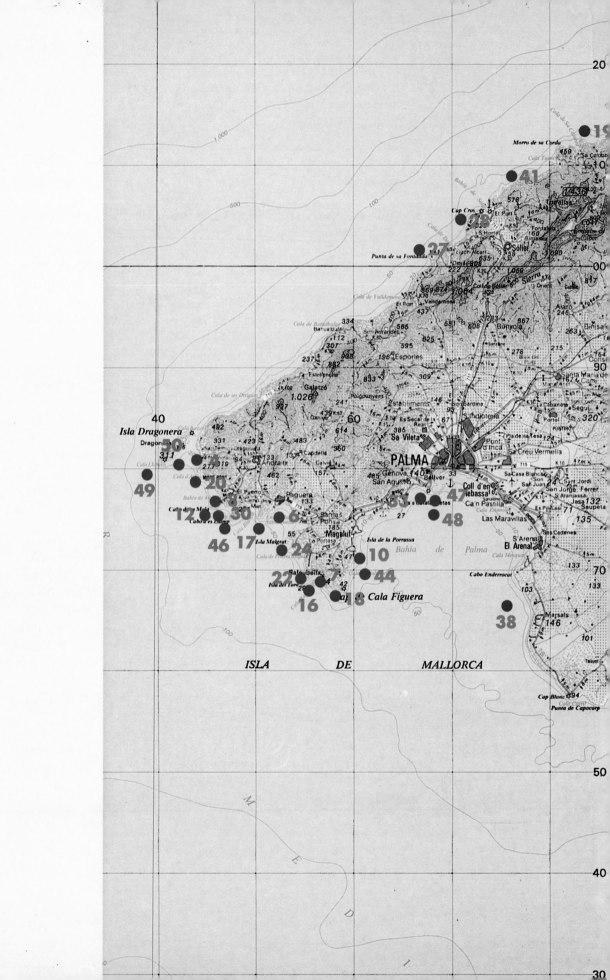

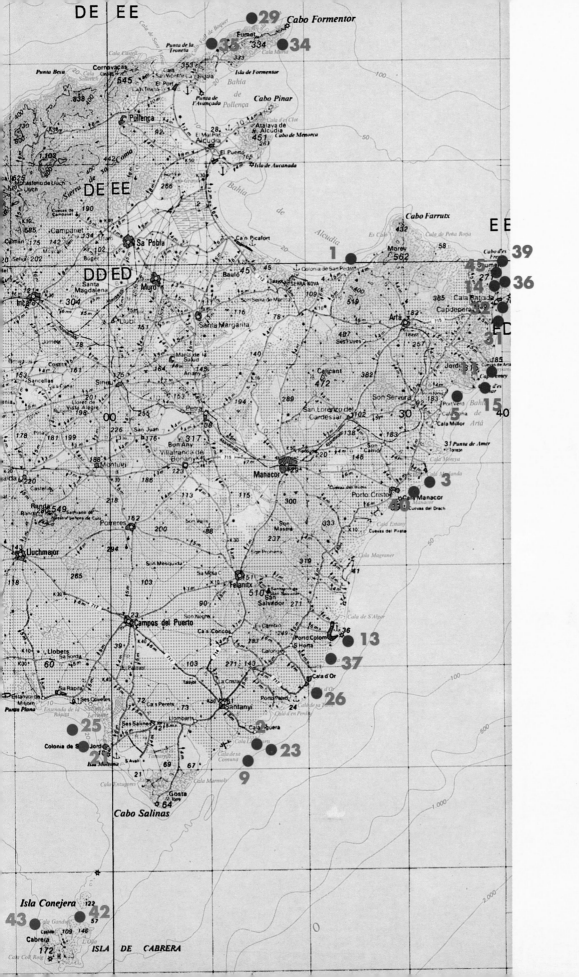

PREFACE

Dear reader, here you have the result of some years of work, hundreds of dives around the coast of Majorca, and many hours sitting in front of the computer to tell you about them; most of all, you have a work done with the care and effort of men and women who share the same passion: the underwater world.

The main object of this book is to offer a guide of dives around the island of Majorca, with the guarantee that our sea is one of the places that offers more possibilities to enjoy non-professional diving. We are assuming that the reader of this guide is an experienced diver, who knows how to behave under the water and who has all the requirements needed by law to practice this sport.

But we have aimed to reach a wider scope of readers: our wish is to show the beauties of our sea to any sensitive person: this is why we have taken care of the aesthetic side of the book, and we have illustrated it with the best photographs we have been able to obtain. We hope that in this respect, the book completely satisfies you, and even more, if you have the right physical conditions and have never practised scuba diving, we would love you to have a go and experiment this new sensation.

Nowadays we can all "breathe" under the sea, reaching places that were absolutely unthinkable only fifty years ago. A happy coalition between technique and nature allows us to have an intimate relationship with the sea. Nobody remains indifferent after the first diving lesson. After breathing under the water everything seems different. Even life above earth becomes easier to endure. Under the tranquil waters, in peaceable flotation, among the light beams that go through the waves and reach us, the peace and self control increase, sensations and qualities that later stay for ever in some corner of our mind.

On the other hand, each year the autonomous scuba diving equipments become lighter, cheaper and safer. There is no doubt that the advances in this sport are growing, but their beneficial effects vanish when certain basic rules are not followed. Whatever happens, you must always follow scrupulously a series of basic safety measures, almost all of them related to the fact that you have to breathe air which is compressed by the increasing pressure that water exerts as you increase your depth. It is therefore crucial to start diving only after having obtained the necessary qualifications through the appropriate non-professional diving courses required by law. You will be qualified to fully enjoy the sea only after obtaining these qualifications.

Contrary to other sports, in scuba diving you must not aim to swim faster, higher or deeper; you want to become better every day. And who is the best diver? It is my opinion that the best diver is the one who helps the others on the boat before diving, the one who without pretension advises the less experienced divers, who never boasts about great depths and has a high sense of friendship and solidarity. The good diver knows his own limits and also the sea's limits; knows which is the right moment to start the return, and even when it is not advisable to even enter the water if the conditions are not right. Without ever forgetting a fundamental rule of behaviour: the respect for the life of the sea inhabitants, something that law requires and common sense recommends, because without life around us the dive loses most of its attraction. You will have the opportunity to observe the difference of visiting the protected area of Cabrera, where the marine fauna vibrates magnificently.

If these rules are met, diving is a very gratifying experience that helps us feel good about ourselves in every sense. Our wish to share these sensations and experiences with you was the reason that drove us to offer you this guide, with the satisfaction of one who shows his most cherished treasures, and with the hope that you will treat them with the respect and admiration they deserve.

Juan Poyatos

THIS IS MAJORCA

The Balearic Islands are about 100 Km away from the Cap de la Nau in Alicante and 150 Km away from Barcelona city. The archipelago is made up of five main islands and a large number of islets, around 190.

Majorca is the largest and most important island of the Balearic archipelago, it has a surface of 3,640 square kilometres and a resident population of about 600.000 inhabitants (in summer the population may double).

Majorca's extension is not very large, but its landscape is very diverse and around its coast (it has a perimeter of about 350 kilometres) you find beaches, coves, steep cliffs, important ports, torrents and all sorts of orographic features characteristic of the western Mediterranean coast.

Within the island, two great areas are differentiated according to their topography: a mountainous part, known as the Serra de Tramuntana, and a practically flat part, known as Es Pla. The extension of the Serra de Tramuntana is approximately 90 kilometres long with a northeast alignment, starting from the town of Andratx up to the town of Pollença. The highest peak in these mountains is Puig Major (1,445 metres), which gives the island a higher average height than that of the United Kingdom. Of course, the entire north coast, dominated by the rugged Serra de Tramuntana, is a compendium of coves and gigantic cliffs. To the abruptness of the north coast we must add the special northern position and the influx of the waters and currents of the gulf of León. With all this, Majorca is a characteristic area for navigation and scuba diving.

In the west side of Majorca, plains and lightly accentuated graceful depressions predominate, which is why the coasts are full of coves with remarkably clear and tranquil waters. Curiously, during the summer they are not so clear and tranquil.

The most characteristic winds – which, more than lashing, they refresh – that blow in Majorca are: Tramuntana, blowing from the north and of far away continental origin, and the Embat, a thermal wind particular to these coasts and specially to the bay of Palma. The Embat wind originates from the temperature difference between the land and the sea, in relation with the sun's influence in summer. The Embat blows from the sea towards the coast during midday, it is quick to form and can cause serious damage to sailors, particularly if they navigate close to the coast, because the wind blows and pushes towards land and causes the so-called "broken" waves.

It is particularly advisable to always consult the meteorological forecast services before deciding on the place you want to head for to spend your diving day. Generally, we can say that in Majorca, when the wind is blowing from one side, the opposite side will be to leeward and therefore calm or at least it will have better weather conditions, except of course when there is a general tempestuous sea. The annual average temperature fluctuates between 13 and 18 degrees centigrade. Rainfall oscillates between 300 and 1,300 mm. per year. Because of its particular orography, Majorca allows for different microclimates, for instance in the Tramuntana mountains the annual rainfall can reach 1,400 mm., while in some eastern areas it barely rains a few times a year.

The land flora of Majorca is relatively limited,

and 'only' around 1,500 species are registered. Insularity has caused a limited variety of fauna and flora, but on the other hand it has allowed for endemic varieties to develop, even within the different islands and islets. Majorca's vegetation has endured the human pressure for thousands of years, 50% of the island's extension is cultivated and the highest mountainous area has a deficiency of rich soils that can be used by the plants. The higher peaks of the Tramuntana mountains are nevertheless where more endemic plant species are registered (approximately 100). The Balearic oak, which once covered the whole island, thrives below 1,000 metres of height. *Quercus ilex*, the common oak, dominated the soil of Majorca when the first inhabitants of the island settled, but the invasion of pines and the proliferation of agriculture in Majorca and stockbreeding in Minorca were responsible for the disappearance of a large part of the oak woods, which also have fire retarding properties. Vegetation on the sandy coastal areas is greatly reduced because of the sea's influence and because of the urban aggression of the eminently tourist coast.

The land fauna is made up of birds, mammals, amphibians and reptiles. Birds are the most abundant of the land animals, reaching 300 species. The mammal group has about 22 species, half of which are bats (represented in the coat of arms of Palma). Reptiles are perhaps the most mysterious inhabitants of the islands; there are snakes, tortoises, and most of all lizards, of which there are endemic subspecies in most of the islets that surround the larger islands.

We must point out the high salt content of the Mediterranean sea, it reaches 38 per thousand, which is equivalent to say that there are 38 grams of salt in every litre of water. The water temperature oscillates between 13 and 26 degrees centigrade during the warmest months. Most of the species that reproduce in these waters live within the first 50 metres of depth. The sea floor of sand, sea-weed and mud predominates between 50 and 100 metres of depth, where life is not very abundant but where you will find lobsters, red mullets, goldmackerels, etc. At lower depths – there are marine basins of nearly 3,000 metres near Cabrera – you can fish squid, swordfish, mackerel sharks and other pelagic species. Nevertheless, the zone between 0 and 50 metres of depth is without a doubt the most interesting; particularly for most of the non-professional divers, the most suitable area to contemplate all kinds of marine species is the area between 20 and 30 metres of depth. In this area, all the characteristic species of the Mediterranean sea are found; combers, octopuses, moray and conger eels, scorpionfish and many others make up the submarine panorama together with the filtering organisms and sedentary predators like corals, sponges, sea whips, wreathy-tufts, anemones, etc. The beauty of these Mediterranean waters however, does not lie only in their fauna and flora: their extraordinary luminosity and the colour that the abundant light provides allows for great dives. The crystal-clear water, specially in Cabrera and Formentor, allows to dive in a unique sea of shades and contrasts.

CABRERA... DIVING IN CRYSTAL CLEAR WATERS

The archipelago of Cabrera lies at the south of Majorca, at about six miles from Cabo Salinas. It is made up of eighteen islands and islets, of which the island of Cabrera is the most important. Despite its small surface (1,569 hectares) and because of its irregular geography, it has a considerable perimeter of 38 kilometres of coast.

The archipelago can be reached by boat from the ports of Sant Jordi, S'Estanyol and La Rápita, and the approximate distance from these ports to the port of Cabrera is between 10 and 13 miles.

On the route from Majorca to Cabrera you are likely to see dolphins, swordfish, and even tuna fish, tortoises or maybe a shark.

The isolation and the abundance of islets have originated the development of interesting ecosystems that hold a diverse and, in some of the islets, endemic fauna, such as some endemic lizard species (*Podarcis lilfordi*).

Ornithology lovers find their paradise in the abundance of marine birds, rare in other places, such as the Audouin's gull (*Larus audouinii*), the shag (*Phalacrocorax aristotelis*) or the osprey or fish eagle (*Pandion haliaetus*).

Cabrera is arid and lacks large green extensions with vegetation along its irregular and steep coast line. However, it has its own plant species and in the smaller islands there are endemic plants that do not exist in the larger ones. Curiously, the abundance of birds in the uninhabited islets allows plant species to thrive and propagate, nourished by the natural manure that the birds drop. The largest Mediterranean marine birds are the Cory's shearwaters (*Calomectris diomedea*), which can reach 1.20 metres of wingspan

and live out at sea, nesting in the rock crevices of the islets near Cabrera.

At the southeast of the island there has long been an imposing tower made out of branches which serves as a nest for the osprey. Every year the couples rear their eaglets in this nest, which is built and rebuilt each season. The singular shape of this nest has given name to the cliff of Niu de S'Àguila (the eagle's nest). This great eagle dives from the air into the sea fishing for food for its offspring. On the other hand, the Eleonora falcons come back every summer from far away Madagascar to nest in Dragonera and Cabrera. The male offers presents to its partner in the shape of succulent insects. The good gallant helps later to rear the offspring and to feed its family with small birds of passage that stop during their migratory flight for a few hours in the island... or for ever in the falcon's nest.

The land vegetation, with around 450 species, is mainly made up of the characteristic Mediterranean maquis, which in the more sheltered areas slowly gets covered with pines.

However, the most extraordinary thing about the national park of Cabrera lies in the crystal clear waters that surround the archipelago. The sea floor is diverse and is made up of large sandy areas and oceanic posidonia beds. The posidonia beds, which are generally mistaken for seaweed, act as a submarine forest, preventing the degradation of the sea floor and protecting it from being eroded by the currents.

As for the marine fauna, it is difficult to mention only one particular species, although the large quantity of groupers of all sizes may be surprising. Groupers are a lot more abundant since

The port of Cabrera. (Photo: C. Huerta)

1991, when the archipelago was declared National Maritime and Land Park for its exceptional environment and landscape values. The different areas and levels of legal protection determine the use of the park. The law which the park is subject to, specifies that it is necessary to have prior permission to sail, anchor or dive around Cabrera. Permission is given at the offices of the park in Palma de Mallorca, where they also inform you in detail about other aspects and activities that take place at the park.

The water in the archipelago of Cabrera is so transparent that it can only be compared to some tropical seas. Because of the special characteristics of these waters (great depth, currents and lack of sheltered areas) it is wise to enquire about the sea conditions beforehand at the diving centres which regularly organise dives in Cabrera. Ideally,

dives should be done within a group outing organised by any of the diving centres or non-professional diving clubs in Majorca.

The park's administration plan contemplates the rotation of the authorised diving areas; today, one of the most recommended dives is Cala Galiota, near 'the friend's cave', where one of the thousands of French prisoners who were confined there in subhuman conditions during the War of Independence (1808-1814), invited a new 'friend' from time to time and then proceeded to eat him.

At the northwest of Cabrera island (southwest coming from Majorca) is Cap de Llebeig, at the highest point of which is the port's lighthouse. It is a steep cape, and it is eroded by the sea and the winds... The bottom of the sea is just as wild.

At some tens of metres or so south of Cap Llebeig is Cala Galiota. You may anchor in this attractive cove and start the dive over a sea floor of steep slopes and large rocks inhabited by small and medium sized groupers. You swim perpendicularly to the coast, until you are about 15 or 20 metres away from the wall. From there, and if the currents are favourable, head towards the south, gaining depth. 30 metres can be reached very easily at the cove, specifically near some rocks at the bottom opposite the large rock that encloses the cove. If you descend very stealthily you may be able to see one or two really large groupers.

The groupers here are still startled at the presence of divers, and you enjoy seeing them this way in their wild and natural state, hunting or swimming without apparent interest in you. You start the way back heading northeast, losing depth. The area is full of groupers everywhere, as if they were damselfish, specially during the summer, and the smaller ones follow the divers with curiosity. Among the groupers are white breams, two-banded sea breams and black breams. You must also keep an eye on the surface and to the visibility limit, which may be of 50 metres, to be able to see barracudas, giltheads, and amber Jacks that also show some interest in divers. Close to the coast you must do a security stop, enjoying the abundant fauna within the cove.

All in all you can say that the visit to Cabrera offers three nearly independent satisfactions: the navigation, the land fauna and the crystal clear waters and abundant groupers around the archipelago's coast. You must not however let the transparency of the water make you forget the depth: the water currents and the changes in the sea have to be watched closely.

Lastly, remember that in Cabrera one must not chase the fish, they will cautiously approach you on their own.

THE WILDEST DIVE... SA DRAGONERA

Sa Dragonera belongs to the municipality of Andratx, and it is the most southwest portion of land of Majorca. With an area of 228 hectares and its highest point at 360 metres, it is a relatively large islet. It has a long contour and its curious name may be due to the shape of a 'sleeping dragon' that it has. Its coast is full of spectacularly steep cliffs, and has many bird species. Important colonies of Eleonora falcons (*Falco eleonorae*), Shags (*Phalacrocorax aristotelis*) and Manx shearwaters (*Puffinus puffinus mauritanicus*) live in Sa Dragonera.

The extension of this islet, which was recently purchased by the Consell Insular de Mallorca after the previous owners made an attempt to develop it, has changed during its history. 4,000 years ago the sea level was four metres higher than it is today, and 25,000 years ago the Mediterranean sea was 100 metres lower than it is now.

Today Dragonera is uninhabited, but anciently it was a kind of sacred island for the first Majorcans. In La Cova de Sa Font (the cave of the fountain), where there is fresh water, some human remains were discovered which could be some 4,000 years old.

Sa Dragonera played an important role in the history of Majorca, serving as a refuge for the Christian fleet of James the first when he started the conquest of Majorca.

Around its coast there are the remains of wrecks from all periods. Today it is still a dangerous place because of the 'needles' at the bottom of the channel of Sa Dragonera; these needles appear and disappear with the waves, forming a deadly trap for boats. If you get close to or dive near the needles you will be able to see clearly the paint marks on the rocks above the water. It is paint from the boats that crash or brush against the channel's needles.

The currents and the great depth in some areas —in Cap Llebeig, only 20 metres away from the cliff's shore there are more than 50 metres of depth— make SA Dragonera a paradise for non-professional divers.

The sighting of large pelagic fish and marine mammals around Sa Dragonera allows you to wonder about the identity of all sorts of usual 'giants' in these waters. Some sperm whales, dolphins, pilot whales (called 'cap d'olla' in Majorcan) and all sorts of deep sea swimmers such as swordfish, red tuna, mackerel, sharks and of course, tortoises, have been catalogued. Apart from pelagic animals, in the depths of Sa Dragonera you find a large number of residents of areas with clean currents such as sponges, sea whips, corals etc. Accompanied always, in the clearest waters, by the characteristic nudibranchial species of the Mediterranean, such as *Hervia costai, Peltodoris atromaculata* and many other of these curious gastropod molluscs that have lost their protective shell during their evolution.

However, without doubt, the divers' main attraction for the Dragonera area is the so-called "conger dive".

The conger eels are located between Sa Dragonera and the port of Sant Elm, and they are the most extreme experience for a non-professional diver in Majorca. This adventure must only be attempted by highly experienced divers. Its risk lies not only in the depth or the adversity of the sea in the channel; its main difficulty is the extreme aggressiveness of the gigantic congers and morays that swim among the remains of a sunken boat. The experience is unforgettable and many are the divers who, having dived among sharks in far away waters, consider the conger dive in Sa Dragonera the most 'adrenaline flowing' of all.

The anchoring is done near the islet, but the sensation is that of being in the open sea. Whenever possible, it is wise to take one adequate boat plus one extra fast boat, to evacuate any unfortunate injured as fast as possible. This is not an exaggeration. Many a diver have gone back with the souvenir of a nasty eel bite. The worst aggression which, according to a reliable source, happened during this dive was when a foreign female diver was bitten on the cheek by a two meters long and forty kilos of weight conger. The hole was so big that the air of the regulator was lost through the wound, without entering her lungs. Only the great professionalism of the instructors who were with her avoided a fatal outcome.

It must be said that, at 30 metres of depth, a panic attack among the divers can cause more injuries than the bites of the moray and conger eels.

The congers – more than 20 live there among large morays– get out of their holes to approach the divers when they see them descending. An expert instructor should feed them from afar and, when they are full of fish, it is possible to get closer to them, but they are not always willing to wait, and the great congers and morays can rush towards the bubbling visitors who arrive with their 'breakfast'. The problem is that sometimes they confuse their food with the hand that offers it.

The experts say that the food carried on the hand must be released before the eels get to us. My own experience is that... there is no time!

I do think it is wise to warn you, if you do the conger dive with a usual diver of the area: see if he has a photographic camera. If he does, he might tell you to go down with the food for the congers, explaining that his hands are busy with the camera and that there is no real danger, that once you get down there he will take the food bag and feed the congers. Do not believe him, what this unscrupulous *cicerone* really wants is to take some spectacular photographs of the congers while they "devour" you.

COLÒNIA DE SANT PERE. CALÓ DES CANS

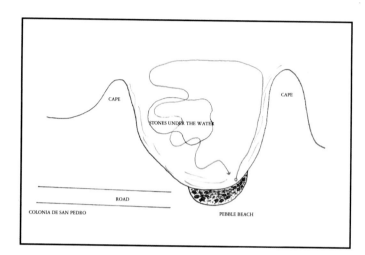

Technique:	very low
Average depth:	6 metres
Maximum depth:	10 metres
Duration:	80 minutes
Difficulties:	next to none
Recommended season:	spring; cuttlefish get close to the coast to spawn

Caló des Cans is at the north of the island, near the Colònia de Sant Pere, in the bay of Alcudia, between the towns of Can Picafort and Cala Ratjada.

This is a very easy and low risk dive, which can also begin from the coast. The depth never reaches the level at which you would have to stop for decompression. Therefore it is a suitable dive for beginners and for children, or also to start the diving season. If it is done by night however, it becomes a different story.

The cove is accessible by car and it is only a couple of hundred metres away from the Colònia

de Sant Pere, following a dirt track at the north of the town.

After equipping yourselves on land, start the dive on the right hand side of the cove. The depth increases as you get further away from the pebble beach of Caló des Cans. Following the right side, or north side of the cove, you get to the end of the shelter. At the entrance you turn to the left to swim over the posidonia bed which covers the Caló's exterior part.

Swimming towards the opposite side of the cove, you will see that the bottom is sandy and rocky, with areas of posidonia where saupes and saddled breams feed.

Right: Beadlet anemone (*Actinia equina*). Common in the north coastal area. (Photo: A. Alonso)

Left: Fan mussel (*Pinna nobilis*). The largest bivalve of the Mediterranean. It used to be very abundant, but today it is rare because its large valves were a trophy for unscrupulous divers and swimmers.

When you are approximately in the centre of the cove's entrance by sea, head towards the pebble beach, swimming underwater at more or less 8 metres of depth.

In the middle of the Caló des Cans you find an enormous area of rocks which are full of galleries, small caves of different shapes, all of this at only 6 metres of depth.

It is here, in the middle of the cove, where you enjoy an exceptionally tranquil dive, very easy and not in the least dangerous.

There isn't much marine life, but in a spring or summer's mid-afternoon, you will be able to observe lots of large cuttlefish.

These cephalopods are not easy to distinguish from the bottom of the sea, that is why it is preferable to start the dive in the late afternoon, or even at night, when you can best observe these "moving stones".

Cuttlefish allow divers to get very close to them. If you hold your breath as you approach them, you will nearly be able to touch them, very gently extending your hand to them. Cuttlefish observe you face to face, almost defiant, showing off their swimming skills and mimetic qualities in front of your eyes. If you stay still, not making any sudden movements and breathing very gently, the cuttlefish will approach you in a very light, nearly transparent colour. When it decides it has come too close or that it hasn't liked one of your movements, it swims backwards and changes to a darker colour, or even swims away propelling itself at great speed and ejecting it black ink.

Easy dive, adequate to see a lot without risk.

Peacock wrasse (*Symphodus tinca*). During the spawning season it is normal to see the males of this species transporting seaweed to build nests in the rock. If after you catch one you return it to the sea, it will find its way back to its nest from considerably far distances of even hundreds of metres. (Photo: C. Huerta)

CALA SANTANYÍ. THE CLEAREST WATERS

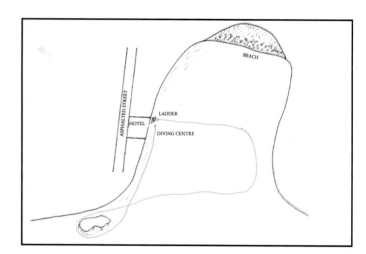

Technique:	low
Average depth:	10 metres
Maximum depth:	14 metres
Duration:	60 minutes
Difficulties:	boats
Recommended season:	spring

Cala Santanyí is probably one of the most beautiful dives around the Majorcan southeast coast.

More information about the area is available by contacting the diving instructors at the Club Albatros diving centre; there they will inform you about the conditions of the sea and the area, and they will advise you about the best ways to carry out the dives in the southeast coast of the island.

You commence the dive from the stairs at the diving centre, just below the Hotel Pinos Playa. You descend only about 5 metres and then cross over the cove in the most beautiful crystal clear waters.

On the cove's sea bed, of clean and very white sand, you may see red mullets, saupes and, occasionally, some annular breams feeding.

When you get to the opposite side of the cove, approximately 30 metres away from the club, you dive following the rocky wall, heading towards the sea. The depth never exceeds 15 metres, and the water is usually so clean and clear that the tourists can observe the dive from the coast rocks and see the divers advancing at ease along the bottom of the sea.

Before you get to the outside of the cove, turn around to cross Cala Santanyí once again, heading towards the coast, until you arrive below the Hotel Pinos Playa.

Suggestive picture of Cala Santanyí with the Albatros club at the back

Crossing over the cove, not far from the sand and the posidonia bed, there is a very good visibility. The bottom of the cove is during some seasons full of wide-eyed flounders, hiding under the sand. Also, in September and October, you may see rays during their mating and laying season. These rays may be of considerable size, and they have a sting at the end of their tail. Rays will not usually attack, but it is advisable not to try and touch them, because the poisonous sting causes great pain in the affected area.

Once you get to the most southern end of the cove, at approximately 12 metres of depth, continue swimming along the bottom, under the small cliff.

Beyond the south point of Cala Santanyí, at which point you will be able to see the entrance to some caves that are described in another chapter, continue diving at 14 metres of depth until you come out of the cove by its right hand side.

At 50 metres from the right side of the cove there is what the locals call "el champiñón" (the mushroom). It is an enormous rock a few metres away from the coast, and it is famous for the exuberant marine life that surrounds it. "The mushroom" is populated by black scorpionfish, large scaled scorpion fish, white breams and all sorts of small crustaceans that provide food to groupers and moray eels.

This dive, a very good one for those who do not have a boat and have to start from land, is quite spectacular when it is done by night, then you may see cuttlefish, nocturnal octopuses, squid and all sorts of flat fish.

1. Cuttlefish (*Sepia officinalis*). It lives over sea beds with sand, pebbles and seaweeds and in marine phanerogam plateaux. It is very frequently seen during the spawning season (spring). 2. Wide-eyed flounder (*Bothus podas*). It lives in sandy bottoms, camouflaging with the substrata, if it senses danger it buries itself under the sand with a swift movement. 3. Common sting-ray (*Dasyatis pastinaca*). One of the largest rays in the Mediterranean. (Photos: A. Alonso). 4. Cleaver wrasse (*Xyrichtis novacula*). Another habitué of the sandy sea bottoms in summer, it spends most of the winter buried under the sand. (Photo: C. Huerta)

CALA MORLANDA THE SANDY COVE

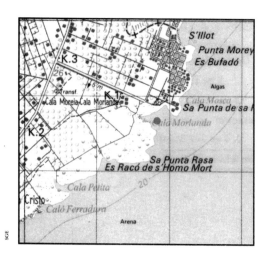

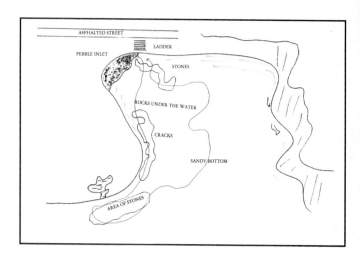

Technique:	low
Average depth:	4 metres
Maximum depth:	6 metres
Duration:	60 minutes
Difficulties:	none
Recommended season:	spring

Cala Morlanda is near Sa Coma, between Cala Millor and Porto Cristo. It is a cove with a rocky beach which is usually clean and has good visibility. You can get to the end of the cove and to the water by car.

There are many diving possibilities here, and one of them is diving to the caves of its south side.

The caves of Cala Morlanda are easy to do and are full of the life that usually populates the great underwater caverns. The cave ends in an open vault with breathable air, but it is advisable to attempt it only with an experienced diver who knows it.

You may want to do this dive with members of the Albatros diving centre, in Cala Millor. In any case, it is always wise to get more details and information about the sea conditions and the state of the cove before entering it.

As you go into the water in Cala Morlanda, you notice its habitually clean and crystal clear waters. Dive heading towards the exit of the cove following the course of the small cliff on the right. Heading towards the way out of the cove, keep the sand to your left and the rocks of the small cliff to your right.

Depth increases but never exceeds 8 metres. As you get close to the cove's exit, you see how

1. The exploration of undersea caverns requires considerable expertise as a diver, as well as having suitable equipment. Still, it is advisable not to enter the caves further than the reach of the entrance's light. 2. Rock blenny (*Parablennius gattorugine*). Small and charming inhabitant of the island's north coast (Photos: A. Alonso).

Padina pavonia. Brownish-grey seaweed, common in shallow waters. (Photo: A. Alonso)

the marine life that inhabits the rocks increases gradually.

Just at the end of the cove, under the point of the small cape that closes Cala Morlanda on its right side, at 6 metres of depth you find the entrance of the cave. It is important to bear in mind that you must not enter the cave (this cave or any cave, for that matter) without adequate preparation and equipment. A metallic cross on the surface, under the cliff, is there in memory of a diver who died when he tried to enter the cave in apnoea.

There are abrupt areas, small caves, holes and rock arches all along the right side of Cala Morlanda. If you are not too scandalous you will be able to see large meagres, goldcrests, *Blenniidae*, *Gobiidae* and maybe one or two solitary fork beards.

Cala Morlanda is a very easy dive that starts at land. It is ideal for diving courses or diving events. It can also be a good outing to do by night.

The sandy bottom between the cliffs at both sides of the cove lends itself to do all sorts of exciting and varied dives, but they may not be so attractive for the more experienced divers. However, the "pure" diver will find this dive a very easy and relaxed one.

SANT ELM. AROUND TO THE PANTALEU ISLAND

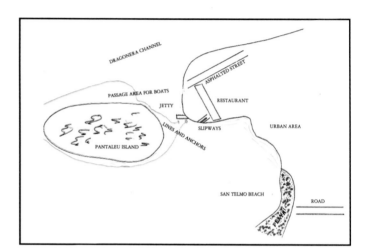

Technique	low
Average depth:	8 metres
Maximum depth:	14 metres
Duration:	50 minutes
Difficulties:	boats during summer
Recommended season:	in summer it lends itself for nocturnal dives

Sant Elm is, at the southwest of Mallorca, the closest town to Sa Dragonera island. This dive can start from the jetty at Sant Elm, it is easy and not too dangerous (except for the maritime traffic). It is also an area where the sea is normally not too rough because it is sheltered by the islands of Pantaleu and Sa Dragonera.

To get to Sant Elm you must drive through Andratx and follow the road to S'Arracó which leads to the beautiful tourist town of Sant Elm. When you get to the beach, go through the town along its main street and continue until you can park close to the jetty which lies at the west end of Sant Elm, facing the island of Pantaleu.

You can get to the jetty by car. Tourist boats called "golondrinas" (swallows) arrive at this small jetty from other ports, moor and disembark. You must be careful and aware of the movements of these boats, they have a considerably deep shaft and the depth of the channel is limited.

At the jetty there is a slipway from where you can launch a boat. Then you can head in the direction of Sa Dragonera, or many other interesting places for non-professional diving, and start to explore. Alternatively, if you do not have a boat, or you simply want to do a practice dive, a dive by night or one for beginners, you can go around the

Feathered worm (*Sabella pavonina*). Sedentary annelid that feeds from the plankton that it captures with its branchial filaments. It usually lives in areas with gentle currents and at any depth. (Photo: C. Huerta)

Pantaleu island, which is only about one hundred metres away from Sant Elm. Pantaleu island was the first place the Christians from James the first occupied during the conquest of Mallorca.

Diving into the water at the jetty, head for the island at a depth of about 6 metres. The sea bottom is of sand and seaweed, and it is saturated with anchors, lines and all sorts of mooring blocks. These blocks make up a real jungle of mooring lines during the summer months. It is important to swim at the maximum depth because boats frequently cruise over your head between the island and Sant Elm.

You circle the island in one direction or the other according to the sea and its currents. It is always preferable to start wherever the sea conditions are worse. The depth is not great, between 6 and 8 metres.

Fan Mussel (*Pinna nobilis*) in a posidonia plateau. It lives in symbiosis with an endemic crab that lives inside it, feeding on the remains of its food. (Photo: J. Serra)

1. *Flabelina affinis* (from 3 to 5 cm long). Eolidaceous nudibranchia. (Photo: A. Alonso). 2. *Dendrodoris grandiflora*. Doridaceous nudibranchia. The epidermic expansions on the back act as secondary gills. Generally these expansions serve as a defence, because in them there are the specialised cells of stinging jellyfish. They feed from these jellyfish among other creatures, and use their specialised cells to defend themselves, placing them inside these expansions. (Photo: C. Huerta)

Red band-fish (*Cepola macrophthalma*), it lives on sandy or slimy sea floors, remaining half buried, in wait for its prey. It has exclusively nocturnal habits and is easy to observe closely if you slowly get close and dazzle it with a torch. It is luminescent white and it usually lives in a group, although individuals tend to maintain a certain distance between one another. (Photo: C. Huerta)

The most interesting area is the channel between the island and the jetty. A curious landscape forms here, because of the quantity of anchors resting on the bottom. In some areas, the current and the sea have exposed wrecks of both old and modern vessels which remind you that this was always a difficult area for maritime traffic, particularly because of the strong currents that surround Sa Dragonera.

All in all, this is a very easy dive that does not involve great risks and that can be very spectacular if you do it at night. As a nocturnal dive it is very impressive because of the great number of cuttlefish that can be seen, even fairly near the coast.

COSTA DES PINS. THE THOUSAND HOLED STONES

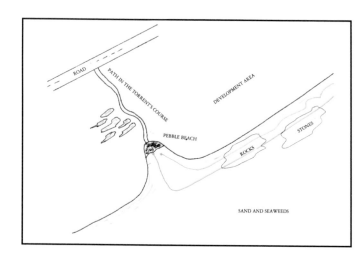

Technique:	low
Average depth:	6 metres
Maximum depth:	9 metres
Duration:	60 minutes
Difficulties:	none
Recommended season:	winter

Costa des Pins is at the north of Mallorca, between Ca'n Picafort and Cala Millor. It is essentially a high standard tourist area and especially during the summer it is visited by many famous people. This coast is specially rich in legends and fantastic stories about shipwrecks and strange events (do not miss any detail during the dives around these places). Very near this place there is the Muertos cove (the Dead's cove) and a sunken wreck known as "pecio de las columnas".

Your diving area is not far from the main road of Costa de los Pinos, in a place known as Punta Rotja.

This is one of the good dives that can start from land, without the need of a boat. Because the water is not very deep and because it is a well sheltered area, it is suitable for practice and learning dives.

The place to enter the water is at the end of a dirt track that comes out on the right hand side of the road, at the entrance of the Costa de los Pinos development. This track is the only direct route to the sea. You can park by the road, alt

1. A group of saupes (*Sarpa salpa*) and flathead grey mullets (*Mugil cephalus*) (Photo: A. Alonso). 2. Green wrasse (*Labrus viridis*) of which there are many subspecies that vary in size and colour. (Photo: A. Torrens).

1. School of saddled breams (*Oblada melanura*). Saddled breams are voracious predators of all sorts of food that floats in the clean waters of Cabrera (Photo: A. Alonso). 2. Ornate wrasse (*Thalassoma pavo*). One of the most dazzling fish in the Mediterranean. It does not fear the divers and it sometimes gets very close to their brightest neoprene suits. (Photo: C. Huerta).

Courtesy of the Banco de Santander (BS).

hough a 4x4 wheel drive vehicle can get right down to the seashore following the track. Accessing the water is easy and quite safe, and the depth increases gradually.

You swim underwater towards the east, parallel to the coast. The depth never reaches 10 metres.

At the beginning, the sea bed is of posidonia, but after no more than 50 metres following the coastline, and to the delight of photographers, a group of large rocks appears in front of your diving masks. There are no spectacular fish species, so you can concentrate on the Painted combers, damselfish, ornate wrasses, saddled breams and sea breams.

Visibility is usually good, and the place is more than adequate for winter dives or to do when the wind is blowing from the north.

The huge rocks, which are only 6 metres deep and a short distance from the seashore, make up complicated shapes that are full of holes and passageways that are safe and easy to explore. There are abundant spiny starfish, red starfish and seasuckers.

It is quite likely that you will not have to stop for decompression and the only difficulty will be to control your buoyancy. A torch is not essential, but it will be of great help to see the friendly groupers who have managed up to now to avoid the underwater fishermen.

The return trip is done going back along the same way, and if the sea is calm and the temperature and visibility are good, you will be able to stay in the water for more than an hour with a 10 litre cylinder.

This place is used regularly by the Albatros diving centre at Cala Millor to initiate beginners to non-professional diving lessons.

All the area that goes from Punta Rotja to Sa Cova des Coloms is suitable for diving as it lends itself for safe dives started from the shore.

CALÓ DES MONJO, THE TUNNEL

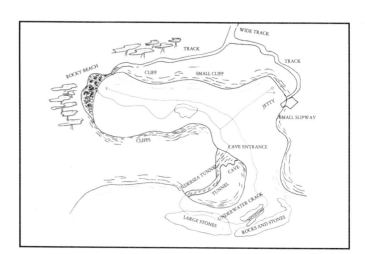

Technique:	low
Average depth:	14 metres
Maximum depth:	18 metres
Duration:	40 minutes
Difficulties:	those of caves
Recommended season:	at day time in winter, taking advantage of a day in which the sea is not suitable for sailing ; at night time in summer.

The Caló des Monjo is a small and beautiful cove at the southwest of Mallorca, close to Peguera, between Peguera and Camp de Mar.

You can do this dive without a boat, starting out from the small pebble beach or the little jetty at the Caló des Monjo. To get to the diving area by car you must take the road from Palma to Andratx, drive through Peguera to the end of the town, where there is a turn to the left indicating the way to Cala Fornells. Following the road to Cala Fornells you will arrive to a restaurant called

Es Verger; at this point you turn to the right onto a paved road, and you follow it until you get to a dirt track which is wide enough for a car.

Follow the track which leads you right into the woods, towards the sea, the track forces you to park when you get to a door on a wall which is covered with signs reading "privado" (private). The place is privately owned, but the access to the sea cannot be restricted, so you walk the rest of the way with your cylinders and equipment. You will have to walk more or less two hundred

1. Caló des Monjo (Photo: C. Huerta). 2. Gigantic octopus (*Octopus vulgaris*) playing with a diver. Some specimens reach three metres and twenty five kilos of weight. (Photo: C. Huerta)

metres until you get to the cove. A 4x4 wheel drive car can get right down to the pebble beach, but it is preferable to leave the car next to the door.

When you arrive to the top of the cliff you will see the cove, then you can either go to the right, towards the small beach, or to the left, towards the little jetty, where it is easier to get geared up and into the water. Whichever way you start, from the beach or from the jetty, the course to take is the same one, bordering the cliff around the right side of the Caló des Monjo. If you get into the water by the "jetty" you must cross the cove to start diving on the right hand side of the small beach. Bordering the cove towards its way out to the open sea, you swim at approximately 8 to 10 metres of depth. Only 200 metres away from the pebble beach there is the entrance to the cave, the Caló's so-called "tunnel". The entrance to this cave is perfectly visible from the surface and the "tunnel" is at approximately 6 metres of depth, on the cliff's wall. The entrance is very wide and normally there are no currents. The "tunnel" is a roughly 25 metres long passageway, the main artery of which turns first to the left and then to the right. Through it, divers can only move one after the other, and the ceiling is only a few centimetres above your head. The bottom is sandy and it is very easy to lift a cloud of sand if you are not careful. Taking a torch is almost indispensable, although some people have been through it without a light, because about halfway through the passage you can already see the light coming from the exit. The cave comes out onto a rocky area. Start the return to the cove staying on the left side. In front of the cove there is a rocky ridge, traversed by another short and lovely tunnel.

All around the cove you may see peacock wrasses, white breams, two-banded sea breams and, at night, squid and one or two nocturnal octopuses.

Good dive, it starts from the shore and it is quite safe to do.

Courtesy of the Conselleria d'Obres Públiques

Prev. Page: Octopus close-up (*Octopus vulgaris*). There are two main species in the Balearics: a nocturnal one (known as red octopus) and a diurnal one.

Over these lines: Comb groupet (*Mycteroperca rubra*). Not a very common Serranidae. It has similar habits to those of the groupers: it is a great territorial predator, it lives inside cracks and caves, and it is more abundant during the summer. (Photos: A. Alonso)

SES BARBINES. THE VIRGIN MALLORCA

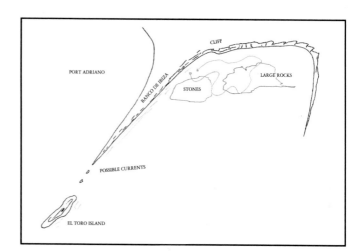

Technique:	medium, low
Average depth:	18 metres
Maximum depth:	28 metres
Duration:	50 minutes
Difficulties:	weather changes
Recommended season:	summer or autumn

The area known as Ses Barbines is very near the El Toro island. It is a rocky wall that goes from El Toro island to the Refaubetx peak.

El Toro island is at the end of the Banc d'Eivissa and from this point, towards the southeast, are Ses Barbines. It is a well suited place for diving, if the sea conditions allow for it. Ses Barbines is ideal to dive when the wind blows from the west or from the south.

The closest port is Port Adriano, and there are a number of diving centres that organise dives around this area, the Unidad Costa Norte and Escuba Palma are there quite regularly.

Finding the ideal place to anchor is not com-plicated at all, you only have to trust your "gut feeling" and anchor in any interesting place between the five hundred metres that separate the point of the Banc d'Eivissa from Cala Refaubetx. Anchoring is easy and the anchor will only go about 10 metres deep.

Start the dive from the anchoring line, then descend directly to the maximum depth, which is about 28 metres. At a certain distance from the cliff you could go down to 40 metres of depth, but that is not your object.

The area of 28 metres of depth is full of large rocks heavily populated by sponges, seaweeds of all kinds, and fish. Between the rocks or under

their dark corners hide black scorpion fish, greater weevers all sorts of conches and wreathy-tufts.

About this expedition, some divers say they have not seen anything interesting; others however, are marvelled with what they see. It is very important to know what to notice and look for. Sometimes the most beautiful thing passes right under or very close to you but you miss it because you do not know what you are looking for.

After a cautious amount of time exploring the rocks at the deepest and farthest part of the cliff, start the journey back "overflying" the bottom which ascends fast amid thousands of stones and holes. Because of the beautiful view, the ascent will be gradual and interesting, and therefore decompression will be "automatic". Heading towards the shore, swim underwater at only a few metres of depth, approaching the boat. You will be amazed by the corals and bentonic organisms that cover the stones and hide between the smallest holes. Explore every corner, every hole or small stone...., there are so many things to see!

them you will be able to see brown meagres and moray eels. Swimming between the large rocks there are white breams and some dentexes, even some gilt-heads and amber Jacks. The most beautiful things to see during this dive are under the large rocks: amid

1. Moray eel (*Muraena helena*). Typical inhabitant of the rocky sea bottoms. Its bite is not poisonous, but the wounds it causes heal very slowly. (Photo: C. Huerta). 2. Snakelocks anemone (*Anemonia sulcata*). Its tentacles produce a skin rash; if you touch them, they adhere so strongly to the skin that they break. (Photo: A. Alonso)

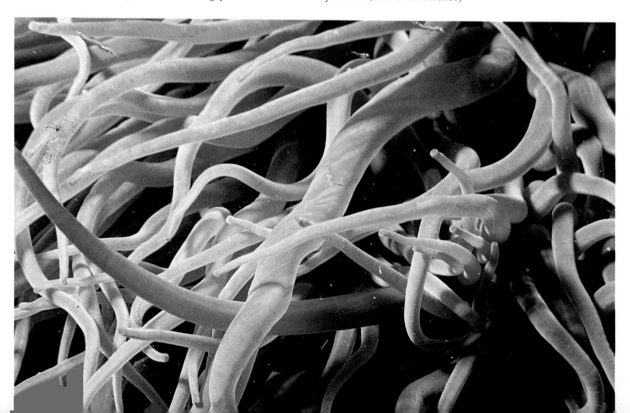

PORT D'ANDRATX. SA MOLA

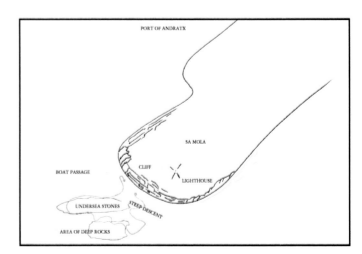

Technique:	medium, low
Average depth:	18 metres
Maximum depth:	20 metres
Duration:	45 minutes
Difficulties:	possibility of rough sea
Recommended season:	in spring or autumn it is an explosion of life

During the right season, the Cabo de Sa Mola is a real explosion of life. The time of the day, the time of the year and/or the sea conditions can cause variations in the fauna of the area, but in normal circumstances, mostly in spring, this is one of the most interesting places of the southwest coast of Mallorca. This is probably what the bottom of the Mediterranean sea looked like originally.

The Cabo de Sa Mola is on the way out of the port of Andratx, towards Santa Ponça. When you get out of the port along its east side it is the first cape you will go around.

It is only possible to access the diving area by boat and the nearest port is, obviously, Andratx.

At the port of Andratx there is a public slipway, from which you can launch a light boat into the sea.

It is also possible to easily get to Sa Mola from Santa Ponça or Sant Elm.

As you come out of the Port of Andratx you see the imposing cape of Sa Mola, where many of the island's VIPs have built their main residences. Start the dive at the end of the mooring line, approximately over the coordinates: I 39-31,9 SN and L 002-2,2 E. The boat will have to stay a few metres away from the steep and rugged cliff.

We start the dive at approximately 12 metres of depth, close to the rocky wall. At the bottom

51

of the sea there are large, scattered rocks inhabited by white breams.

Continue towards the west following the cliff. It is not necessary to descend too much, since the most interesting fauna is between the underwater cliff and its edge on the water surface. You will be able to see moray eels, groupers, dentexes and possibly some mock pollacks.

It is important to keep your eyes wide open, and not only looking at the sea floor, because barracudas, sea basses and dentexes will be observing you from the point where blue turns into grey, at your visibility limit.

The encounter with the great dentex can be memorable. It is wise to remember that instead of trying to get closer to it, it is preferable to stay motionless, nearly holding your breath, holding onto a rock or in the middle of the water, looking at it distractedly. The great dentex may cautiously get closer to investigate and observe the divers, but always at a cautious distance and ready to disappear within a fraction of a second.

When the manometer indicates that you have approximately half of the air left, you must start to return, ascending slowly as you swim towards the east, bordering the edge of the underwater cliff.

On a lucky day, the point of Sa Mola cape can only be compared to a diving experience in the island of Cabrera for the amount of marine fauna found in it.

1. White bream (*Diplodus sargus*). It reproduces from April until June, and like the rest of hermaphrodites, it is first male and then female. (Photo: A. Alonso). 2. Brown meagre (*Sciaena umbra*), it lives only in deep and dark cracks and in groups that can be very numerous. They do not usually go very far from their habitat of large rocks. (Photo: A. Torrens)

CALA LLOMBARDS. THE GROUPERS' ROCKS

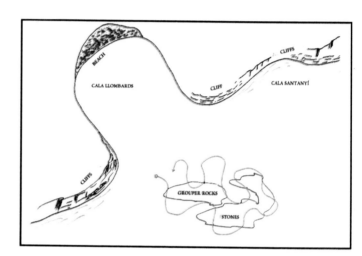

Technique:	low, medium
Average depth:	18 metres
Maximum depth:	22 metres
Duration:	45 minutes
Difficulties:	anchoring and weather changes
Recommended season:	early hours of the day in summer, before the "embat" starts to blow

Cala Llombards is very close to the town of Santanyí, but it will be better to start the dive from the Albatros diving centre, in Cala Santanyí.

From there, scuba diving excursions to the area of Cala Llombards are organised constantly during the summer months. In winter, a boat on a trailer can be launched from the beach into the water.

The area of the "rocks", where a trap-net is installed in summer, is approximately half a mile away from Cala Llombards and one mile away from Cala Santanyí.

It is necessary to access the area by boat. Anchoring is quite difficult because of possible changes in the weather, particularly during the summer when the thermal winds predominate. At the Albatros diving centre, below the Pinos Playa Hotel, they will inform you about the sea conditions, or even take you to the exact diving area. They can also recommend you other possi-

1. The Brown meagre (*Sciaena umbra*) is between golden and silvery, and it can reach a considerable size. (Photo: C. Huerta). 2. Flying gunard (*Dactylopterus volitans*). Its large "wings" make it one of the most curious and beautiful fish you can observe during the dive. These "wings" are to detect their possible prey under the sand. (Photo: A. Alonso)

1. Family of groupers (*Epinephelus guaza*) (Photo: A. Torrens). 2. Gilthead (*Sparus aurata*). One of the fastest predators of our coasts. It owes its name to a golden spot on its forehead (Photo: C. Huerta). 3. Barracuda (*Sphyraena sphyraena*). Powerful predator that lives and hunts in groups. It has a large and strong mandible with sharp teeth (Photo: A. Alonso). 4. When the grouper (*Epinephelus guaza*) reaches a certain size, it tends to live and hunt alone, becoming more unfriendly and elusive (Photo: A. Torrens).

ble dives in the area between Cala Santanyí and Cala Figuera.

Once at the anchoring spot, descend about 14 metres. The dive must start heading towards "the grouper rocks", which can more or less be seen from the surface. The group of rocks has a radius of 400 metres.

The extension of the "grouper rocks" is so large that one dive is not sufficient to see them completely.

The huge cavities and rocks superimpose and intersect, varying the depth constantly and exposing holes where a large number of groupers of all sizes hide. It is a great dive where it is advisable to take a torch and a photographic camera to take some good pictures.

Corvachos and peacock wrasses accompany the groupers between the rocks. A conger eel or two of considerable size dispute the rocks along with

the octopuses and some moray eels. The life here is really exuberant.

The rocks have to be explored very carefully, without going into the holes abruptly and without interfering with the life of the groupers. Some of the larger specimens look out of their caves to observe the divers, they do not hide or try to flee, ... for the moment.

Apart from the characteristic marine life of this practically virgin territory, there is the added satisfaction of the luminosity of Majorca's east coast and the extraordinary arrangement of the large "grouper rocks".

The course will be as long as you can make it. Depending on the time of the year, you will find more or less marine fauna, but if you know how to search and wait, you may be able to see groupers that still "challenge" the divers face to face.

ISLAND OF EL SEC. THE SUBMARINE

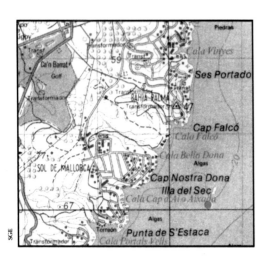

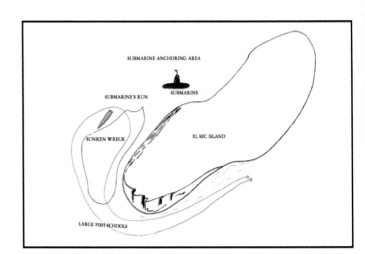

Technique:	medium
Average depth:	20 metres
Maximum depth:	26 metres
Duration:	45 minutes
Difficulties:	the sunken wreck and the weather changes
Recommended season:	winter-spring. In summer the "embat" blows very strongly in this area

The islet of El Sec is in the south coast of Majorca, approximately opposite the casino, near Magalluf and Palma Nova. During the last couple of years it has been used as an immersion area for an electric submarine carrying tourists, this has turned the island into a great and obligatory dive for all scuba divers. During the summer, the submarine stays anchored by the islet and a ferry transports tourists from land to the "Neptuno". The transfer is done a few metres from the islet and the submarine does a 30 minute immersion carrying more or less 40 tourists. For the non-professional scuba diver, to contemplate the sub-

marine during its subacuatic tour is already something quite amazing (it is remarkable to see how the crew skilfully manoeuvre it around the rocks on the sea bottom). But the best thing about this dive is the show that the professional divers hired by the company put on for the visitors. These divers, to the visitors' astonished faces, hand feed the fish around the area. Schools of saddled breams, saupes and annular breams have learned how easy it is to get food when the "metallic monster" submerges. With all the appropriate precautions and without getting too close to the submarine, you will enjoy feeding the

hundreds of fish of all sizes that come to you (do not forget to bring the camera and gloves). Apart from the sensation of being inside a "cloud" of fish, you also have the opportunity to explore a sunken wreck of around 22 metres in length which was sunk on the west side of the islet with the object –truly achieved – of showing the tourists an easy and noteworthy scene of the Balearic sea bottom for their enjoyment.

The islet of El Sec is opposite the Portals Vells cove, exactly one mile away from the coast, with a course of 70 degrees from the entrance of the cove. On the sand of the Portals Vells cove there is a suitable place to launch a small boat, except during the summer. The nearest ports are Palma Nova and Portals.

The Calumet diving centre, at the Bonanza Playa Hotel in Illetas, organises regular dives in El Sec.

When you arrive to the proximities of the islet, and after making sure that you will not be disturbing the submarine in its tour, anchor to leeward. Descend along the anchor line about 14 metres. When you get to the bottom, circle half the islet along the south, that is, swim southwards when you go, and come back northwards. At the southern point of the islet lies the sunken wreck, at about 20 metres of depth. The sunken vessel is for the enjoyment of tourists, it has not been prepared for visits from scuba divers, and some of the structures in its interior collapse.

Some of the deck doors on the wreck entice you to go inside and explore, but, beware!: these doors close very easily, and can trap a diver inside. The large hole on the starboard side is no guarantee to be able to get out of the wreck.

1. White breams (*Diplodus sargus*), Saddled breams (*Oblada melanura*) and bogues (*Boops boops*) (Photo: A. Alonso). 2. Stern of the shipwreck "Klara", sunken near the El Sec islet. 3. Cloud of white breams (*Diplodus sargus*) accepting food from a diver. This fish feeding practice is not very advisable because it can change their natural habits (Photos: C. Huerta)

CANYAMEL, SA BATEDORA DES GEGANT

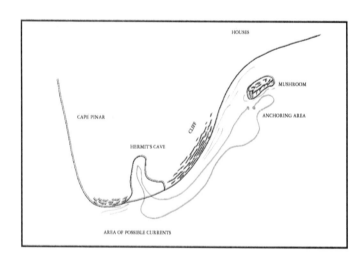

Technique:	low
Average depth:	16 metres
Maximum depth:	19 metres
Duration:	50 minutes
Difficulties:	the caves
Recommended season:	winter-spring

At the northeast coast of Mallorca, between Cala Millor and Cala Ratjada, are Costa des Pins and the beach of Canyamel.

The whole area is very good for scuba diving, and one of the most interesting places is the great crag of Cap des Pinar. This crag separates the bay of Artá and the bay of Canyamel. The immense rocky outcrop of the Cap des Pinar has a succession of small and mysterious caves at its most eastern edge.

The cave of the hermit crabs is one of the many caves you may explore at the point of the Cap des Pinar. In order to get to the anchoring spot you need a boat, which can be launched from the slipway at Cala Bona. The anchoring spot is a

tiny and hardly noticeable cove called Sa Batedora des Gegant (the giant's washboard). At this place there is an outstanding large rock known as the "champiñón" (the mushroom).

You dive into the water not far from the "champiñón", swimming towards the south, looking for the point of the cape Pinar. The cave of the hermit crabs is beneath the enormous rock of the point, it is called like this because of the many easily frightened hermit crabs that live in it. The entrance is not very easy to find, because it is hidden between a group of rocks that seem to hide the cave to protect the crabs.

The cave is not big, but it is an added attrac-

Beautiful fan mussel (*Pinna nobilis*) with a Rainbow (*Coris julis*) swimming over it. The presence of many fan mussels indicates that the waters are clean and that the currents, in which many organic elements can proliferate, are moderate. (Photo: C. Huerta)

1. Hermit crab (*Dardanus arrosor*) in symbiosis with a few anemones (*Calliactis parasitica*). While the anemone protects the crab with its stinging filaments, it also takes advantage of the mobility of its companion, which makes finding food easier. (Photo: A. Alonso). 2. *Crambe crambe* is the most common sea sponge in the Mediterranean. Sponges constitute the group of organisms with the simplest organisation among multicellular life forms, they lack muscles, nerves and sensitive organs (Photo: A. Alonso). 3. Axillary wrasse (*Symphodus mediterraneus*). A solitary Labridae that reaches 17 cm. During May and June the males build nests with seaweeds and sand, and they defend them fiercely, making individuals from other species, even larger that themselves, retreat (Photo: C. Huerta).

tion to the dive. You will have to find the entrance to the cavern and when you do, you will find that it doesn't inspire much confidence. Anybody who wants to enter the cave of the hermit crabs has to have a perfect control of his buoyancy and must not suffer from claustrophobia. The bottom is sandy and it is vital not to shake it up, to avoid panic on the way out. It is impossible to get lost inside it, but it is a good idea to enter in small groups of a maximum of three. In case there is any doubt it is advisable to get more information at the Albatros diving centre in Cala Millor.

This is a good area for an exploration dive and, in spite of the fact that there is not much life, the cave of the hermits and its rocky sea floor, which is full of fan mussels, more than compensate for that. Remember that the fan mussel is a protec-ted species, they are scarce in areas where only a few years ago they lived in large groups of thousands. In the area of Cap Pinar it is still possible to contemplate fan mussels in great quantities. If we very gently approach the open fan mussel, with a bit of luck we may be able to see the beautiful white crab that lives inside the mussel as an endemic parasite. These species have reached a beneficial symbiosis for both. The crab obtains food from the mussel and in turn keeps it clean.

You start the way back going back on your own "steps", and if you have any air left, you can reach the famous "champiñón", where you may see all sorts of filtering organisms. Sponges and other habitués of the currents have established on the rock to take advantage of the constant flow of microscopic nourishment.

PORT D'ANDRATX. S'AGUILOT ISLET

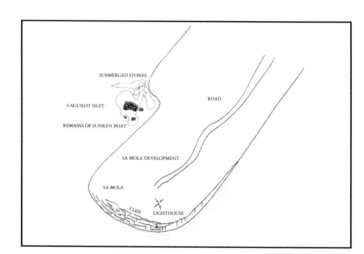

Technique:	low
Average depth:	14 metres
Maximum depth:	22 metres
Duration:	60 minutes
Difficulties:	none
Recommended season:	spring

This is a very easy dive for which you need a boat. During the dive, only two miles away from Port d'Andratx you will see barracudas, giltheads and even lobsters.

Head for Cap de Sa Mola as you come out from Port d'Andratx. Before you get there, just after Punta des Morter, you will find the islet of s'Aguilot. This is a large rock that forms a minute island a few tens of metres away from the abrupt coast of Cabo de Sa Mola. The highest point of the islet, which is at a small cove, is about 15 metres above the sea level. In the water the depth reaches 22 metres.

This dive is suitable as an alternative dive, when for instance, you come out of Port d'Andratx to go diving in Sa Mola, Sant Elm, Dragonera or Cap des Llamp, and the sea is too rough to let you reach these places.

Here you will find quite interesting holes and abundant marine life. The dive is pleasant and involves no great difficulties; furthermore, your boat will be sheltered behind the rock of s'Aguilot. This is possibly the best dive around the Port of Andratx.

The best place for anchoring is between S'Aguilot and the wall of Sa Mola's cliff.

Swim all around the islet starting at the maximum depth, that is, on the southwest side of the

66

Blenny, possibly a *Tripterygion tripteronotus*. Blenniidae and Tripterygiidae are difficult to distinguish. Today scientists are still discovering new varieties of them. (Photo: C. Huerta)

1. Moray eel (*Muraena helena*). It is unusual to see one swimming, like in this picture, out of its hole. 2. Barracuda (*Sphyraena sphyraena*). It is a voracious pelagic predator that can reach lengths of one metre or more. When they are young they swim within very large schools, but as they get larger, they become solitary. They are curious and feel attracted by the divers' presence, they can come closer to them, even to only a few metres away. 3. S'Aguilot, between Sa Mola and Port d'Andratx. (Photo: A. Alonso)

islet, moving against the current along the wall of S'Aguilot. At the part of the islet closest to the cliff of Sa Mola you go inside a great "hole", an ample tunnel which, at only 10 metres of depth, is wide enough for two divers to swim through at the same time.

You may be able to see moray eels throughout the entire southwest side of the islet, and occasionally you might see them hunting down and devouring one of the abundant octopuses around the area. If from the tunnel you move towards the northwest, crossing over a posidonia bed and reaching 20 metres of depth, you will find the remains of a small, very deteriorated vessel inhabited by a few conger eels. In winter you can observe some lobsters and barracudas. Barracudas could be observing you from a distance, at the limit of visibility, generally over your heads, 40 or 50 metres away from you and only one or two metres under the water surface. The strategy to be able to observe them properly (as with practically all the sea inhabitants) is to stay motionless and to look unconcerned about their presence, not approaching them and without making any brusque movements. If the barracuda is curious enough –and that is often the case–, it will swim towards you describing large circles, until it is about four or five metres away, if you are lucky; it is then when you can take pictures if you have a camera ready. Barracudas usually swim in large schools when they are small; later, when they reach a considerable size, they hunt in groups of two or three individuals.

PORTO COLOM. THE LIGHTHOUSE

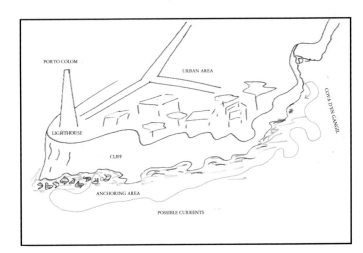

Technique:	low
Average depth:	16 metres
Maximum depth:	20 metres
Duration:	60 minutes
Difficulties:	the thermal wind in summer
Recommended season:	winter or spring

Porto Colom is situated at the southeast of Mallorca and even today it is an important fishing port of long seafaring tradition.

The diving area is on the left hand side, on the way out of the port, very close to the lighthouse that signals the entrance to the inlet. The whole coast is abrupt and under the surface of the water there are plenty of great rocks and submerged walls that run parallel to the seashore. A bit further away from the great underwater cliffs there are large sand banks and posidonia beds.

At the foot of the lighthouse there is a small cove: this is the right place to anchor the boat.

You start the dive after anchoring at the small cove under the lighthouse of Porto Colom. If there is one diver in the group willing to stay on the boat while the others explore for a while, then he or she can leave you at the cove, and the "boatman" can continue towards the northeast while you follow the cliff along the bottom of the sea, approaching the large cave that can be seen from above the water. The "boatman" will collect you after one hundred metres approximately, to then take the boat right in front of the cave.

The best place to visit with the diving equipment is the point of the rock, which is the natural prolongation of the lighthouse. This place is full of large rocks that form an easy to explore

1. The rocks at the foot of the lighthouse are one of the ideal places for diving in the east of Majorca. (Photo: J. Serra). 2. Red mullet (*Mullus surmuletus*), with its barbels it searches for small crustaceans under the sand (Photo: A. Alonso)

1. Cape town lobster (*Scyllarides latus*) one of the largest crustaceans in the Mediterranean, it can reach 5 kilos of weight. It lives in dark areas among caves and cracks. It is present in almost all the seas, although the Majorcan variety has its own characteristics, different even from those in Minorca and Ibiza (Photo: C. Huerta). 2. Sea bottom at the lighthouse of Porto Colom (Photo: C. Huerta). 3. *Cerianthus membranaceus*, it lives on slimy sea floors, its tentacles extend to find food, which is normally plankton, although sometimes also larger organisms, even fish. (Photo: A. Torrens)

and beautiful tunnel. Close to the rocks, a bit deeper, there are some seaweed beds with rainbow wrasses, damselfish, axillary wrasses and other small fish.

Beyond the cove there is a rocky stretch that runs between the cliff and the sandy area with wider and narrower parts. In this rocky stretch there are white breams, combers and a few common octopuses of considerable size. Between the rocks you can also see some large scaled scorpion fish, goldcrests and, with luck, one or two lonely sea horses.

You must not miss the chance to explore the sand and seaweed area, where red mullets scratch around, looking for their food, which consists of larvae and eggs of other species, as well as small crustaceans and molluscs. Also, on the sandy sea bottom, specially during autumn, there are some common sting-rays or electric rays spawning. Observing carefully you might be able to see one or two large anglerfish, lying in wait for their pray on the rocky and sandy sea bottom. Another possible inhabitant of these waters is the Majorcan variety of the Cape town lobster, which is one of the most curious and rare species of the Mediterranean waters. The Cape town lobster usually clings onto the ceiling in rock crevices and caves, it does not like sunlight and you have to use a torch to be able to see it.

CALA AGULLA. SES COVETES

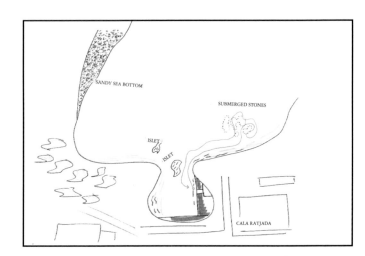

Technique:	low
Average depth:	12 metres
Maximum depth:	17 metres
Duration:	60 minutes
Recommended season:	in autumn the fauna is usually more abundant

In the bay of Cala Agulla, near Cala Ratjada, at the north of the island, there are a number of commendable dives. This one is doubly interesting and attractive for divers who do not like navigating in winter, because you do not need a boat, you can start from the shore.

Some of the best dives you can do around Majorca converge in this area because it is an area of frequent water currents, the waters are very clean, and because the coast of Cala Ratjada has remained relatively undisturbed.

In Cala Agulla there are dives for any level of diving expertise. There are easy or very easy areas, but there are also some caves for the cave diving experts.

The Ses Covetes dive is one of the classic ones, and it occurs among beautiful rocks, which at the bottom form a cavern with a number of tunnel accesses and exits. The maze of holes and passageways does not involve any risk at all, except if a diver attempts to cross a passage which is too narrow.

To get to the diving area of Ses Covetes you must swim from Cala Lliteres, where the Mero

1. Fantastic undersea landscape of Ses Covetes (Photo: C. Huerta). 2. The grouper (*Epinephelus guaza*) seems to be looking at the diver straight into the eyes, retreating slowly towards its cave as you approach it (Photo: A. Alonso)

Coming out at Cala Lliteres, Club Mero (Photo: C. Huerta)

diving centre is. This centre organises outings to a number of areas in the northeast of the island. The more practical minded divers can rent underwater propellants or *scooters* at the Club Mero, and thus save themselves having to swim to Ses Covetes. However, the distance to swim is not too lengthy.

As you move out of Cala Lliteres, along the right hand side, swimming parallel to the coast and at 10 metres of depth approximately, you immediately see the first rock formations, which are only about 50 metres away from the cove.

The first thing you will notice is a great rock in the shape of a hammer, like a huge mushroom.

Then you arrive to a short tunnel. This tunnel leads to a seriously eroded rocky cliff that forms a large vault. Continue along the rock's main axis, under impressive canopies of suggestive shapes,

until you arrive to a narrow bridge. Finally, after swimming over a sandy basin, you reach a large underwater cavern. This is the most beautiful part of the dive and it constitutes a real paradise for underwater photographers.

After exploring the rocks and cavities of Ses Covetes, you have to start the way back along the same route, heading towards the west. But before you leave there is one more cavern to see. It divides into two branches that come out of the main cave. You can enter them, taking care not to reach the dangerously narrow part.

Not far from the point where the dive starts, you may be able to notice groups of saupes, white breams and giltheads.

In summary, a great dive which is very easy and can also be started from the coast, without a boat.

CANYAMEL. CAP VERMELL

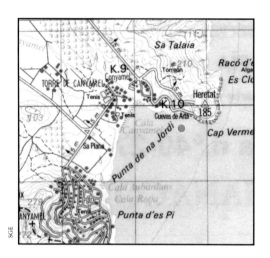

Technique:	medium, high
Average depth:	16 metres
Maximum depth:	24 metres
Duration:	50 minutes
Difficulties:	possible currents
Recommended season:	summer

The beautiful beach of Canyamel is between the bay of Artà and Cala Ratjada. This area, which has been developed in the last few decades, is where the great crag of Cap Vermell looks out onto the sea. The crag is one of the most eastern portions of land in Majorca, and it is influenced by the peculiarities of the sea in this easterly side, that is, its currents and thermal winds. It is called Cap Vermell (red cape) because of its shape and reddish colour, typical of ferrite strata. The inside of the Cap is full of caverns and corridors which delight the tourists that visit the caves of Artà.

From the beach of Canyamel you can launch a pneumatic boat into the water and head towards the point of the cape. The anchoring spot is a few metres away from the cliff and beyond the entrance for tourists to the cave of Artà, which will appear somewhere along the rocks before you.

The most suitable place for diving in this side of the cape is just after the entrance to the cave of Artà, opposite a large rock that looks like a lump on the cliff at sea level, and before arriving to another small cavern that "hangs" from the cliff. The sea bottom all around this territory is suitable for diving, but this is the best area.

For safety reasons it is possible to do this fairly risky dive within one of the groups organised by the Albatros diving centre in Cala Millor, the ins-

BS

1. Small red scorpion fish (*Scorpaena notata*). It lives up to its appearance: touching it can be very painful. It has a great mimetic ability that makes many of them practically invisible among the rocks (Photo: A. Alonso)

tructors of which know the Cap extremely well.

Once you are in the water, take the maximum depth which is approximately 24 metres over some beautiful sand banks. In this part of the sea and during some months of the year – September and October – you can possibly see common sting rays spawning.

Lose depth gradually while you explore the intricate rocks that run parallel to the underwater part of the cliff.

Head towards the east, following the main structure of the Cap.

The rocks are full of holes and small caves where medium-sized groupers swim around. There are abundant large scaled scorpion fish as well as other rock fish, and they seem to play hide and seek with the divers.

Groupers and brown meagres are bewildered at the "fish men's" wanderings, and they tend to get closer to observe the intruders: here the fish are still surprised when they are visited by man.

In some occasions it is possible to observe imposing specimens of barracudas and dentexes swimming freely in the sea, as well as all sorts of nudibranchials and hermit crabs all over the rocks.

Within the area at 14 metres of depth, the dive is particularly luminous around the proximities of the cliff.

You must bear in mind that this proliferation of life is a consequence in many cases of the currents that feed the filtering organisms; because of these same currents you have to program your expedition adequately in order to avoid too much "pedalling" on the way back.

The Cap Vermell, of 185 metres of height above the sea level, points towards the east and it will be a great and unforgettable dive for any diving enthusiast.

Peltodoris atromaculata. In spite of its small size, observing it closely can turn any dive into a special event. Despite its harmless appearance it is an aggressive predator of small organisms which it patiently and slowly devours, holding on to the rocks (Photo: A. Torrens)

Dendrodoris grandiflora. It usually inhabits caves or very dark areas and reaches about twenty centimetres. Because it is almost totally motionless it can go unnoticed to divers with little experience or to those who swim too fast (Photo: A. Torrens).

Close-up of a wide-eyed flounder (*Bothus podas*) photographed by Carlos Huerta, Balearic champion in this modality of undersea photography.

EL TORO. EAST SIDE, THE SCHOOL OF COLOUR

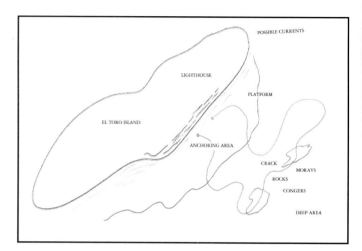

Technique:	diving routes for any level are possible
Average depth:	16 metres
Maximum depth:	45 metres
Duration:	it depends, according to the depth
Difficulties:	possible decompression
Recommended season:	spring-summer

The east side of the El Toro island is the place used by a number of diving centres to perform exercises, courses and all sorts of dives, it is even used to impart professional diving courses.

In El Toro it is possible to take pleasure from all the diving techniques, and it is suitable for any kind of diver, with either a high or a low level of expertise. The different depth levels allow you to program a number of dives according to your own ability, from very easy to difficult.

Anchoring is easy, because there is a sort of underwater platform at about six metres of depth bordering the east side of the islet. There is plenty of life on this platform, and it is possible to do beginner dives or rescue courses around it.

Beyond the platform, the depth of the water starts a gradual descent that reaches and even exceeds 40 metres.

The nearest port is Port Adriano, where the Unidad Costa Norte diving centre is, and where they have their own hyperbaric chamber.

There are various clubs and centres that dive around El Toro island, one of them is Escuba Palma of Santa Ponça, which normally has its boat moored at Port Adriano.

Diving boat at the foot of El Toro islet (Photo: J. Poyatos)

Left: diver surrounded by a school of Saddled breams (*Oblada melanura*) (Photo: C. Huerta)
Above: large groups of amber Jacks (*Seriola dumerili*) hound large schools of smaller fish, combining the speed of their attacks with an apparent hunting strategy (Photo: A. Alonso)

Escuba Palma performs its beginner and advanced diving courses in the east side of El Toro. Unidad Costa Norte is dedicated mostly to training professional divers.

Anchoring on the east side of El Toro is easy, and it allows to stay to leeward if the wind blows from the west. The port of departure is nearby, and the hyperbaric chamber of Unidad Costa Norte is another safety guarantee.

The marine life in this area, the quantity and variety of colours of the corals, seaweeds, sponges and all sorts of species, will allow the first time diver to enjoy an unforgettable memory.

Fearless peacock wrasses, friendly rainbows, thousands of ornate wrasses and some saddled and white breams follow behind the diver to feed on the small organisms that the diver's flippers always lift from the bottom.

Rainbows and ornate wrasses will swim around in front of your goggles, trying to find something edible near you. At the deepest side of the island, at about 40 metres, a group of three large rocks provides accommodation for conger and moray eels of considerable size, who seem to look out of their rocks to observe their enigmatic visitors in bright colours and making noisy bubbles.

Apart from the living creatures who cling to the rocks and the characteristic fish of medium depths in the south coast of Majorca, some habitués of the open sea can sometimes be seen at El Toro. The biologists at the University of the Balearic Islands have registered the passing of groups of dolphins, blue sharks, swordfish, tuna fish, sunfish, and other habitual fish of the depths and the open sea.

CAP ANDRITXOL. THE ROCKS OF LIFE

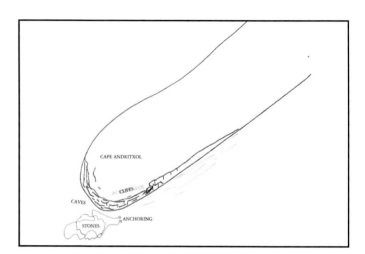

Technique:	medium
Average depth:	25 metres
Maximum depth:	33 metres
Duration:	50 minutes
Difficulties:	the depth and the crevices in the rocks
Recommended season:	winter-spring

At the continuation of the Cap Andritxol there are some gigantic rocks in which marine life proliferates in a most spectacular way. Here it is possible to observe groupers, moray eels, large white breams and even lobsters and conger eels between the crevices and passageways in the rocks that seem to have fallen from the top of the Cap Andritxol.

The nearest port is the Puerto Deportivo Santa Ponça, and the nearest diving centre is Escuba Palma, in the bay of Santa Ponça.

Escuba Palma is a centre specially dedicated to tourists and foreign residents, and apart from the usual services of any other centre, Escuba stands

out for its particular diving modus operandi, which is to never take large groups diving, and this allows the divers to observe the sea better and to concentrate more.

Cap Andritxol is one of the favourite dives for the people who run Escuba Palma, because of its special configuration of large superimposed rocks that allow the marine life to flourish exuberantly.

Leaving the port of Santa Ponça, Port d'Andratx or Port Adriano, you then head towards Cap Andritxol. The enormous volume of the cape does not allow any error when anchoring, and finding a convenient place to start the dive will be easy.

1. Greater weever (*Trachinus draco*). One of the few dangerous fish in the Mediterranean, it has poisonous spines on its dorsal fin and in its operculum (Photo: C. Huerta). 2. Scorpion fish trapped in a trammel. This netting consists of a barrier made up of three nets, two exterior ones with wide meshes and one in the middle with a tighter mesh. When a fish swims through the first mesh, it hits the second one and forms a bag with the third one, from which it can hardly escape (Photo: A. Alonso)

The drop of the anchor will be between 20 and 30 metres. Leave the boat about 40 metres away from the cliff's wall, bearing in mind the swing at anchor and that other boats will pass by quite frequently.

The anchoring spot is in front of a dark coloured sort of cave which is at the end of the Cap Andritxol.

The dive is practically vertical to a depth of approximately 28 metres. At the bottom there are huge rocks, and between the rock crevices there are brown meagres and a few lobsters.

The visibility in the water is usually good, despite the considerable depth. The main difficulty of the sea in this area is the possibility of weather changes, especially at certain times of the day.

Descend following the undersea cliff down to no more than 30 metres. Soon after this there is a posidonia and sand bed, which does not hold much interest. Return more or less over the same route, following the natural progression of the Cap Andritxol. Between the large rocks you can take the opportunity to progressively get rid of some nitrogen.

Between the rocks, which are full of white breams and moray eels, there are remains of drift nets that reveal the fishermen's eagerness to reach these huge rocks that are full of life. This is a passage area for boats during the summer, and there are some pretty brusque weather changes, so you must be very careful when you reach the surface. It is convenient to stay around the rocks near the coast, at the edge of the cliff of Cap Andritxol, for a safe amount of time; there is not a more pleasant place to wait during the decompression.

Wreathy-tuft (*Spirographis spallanzanii*). Tube worm that lives on the rocky sea bottoms. It is capable to detect the waves that divers produce as they get closer, hiding within a fraction of a second inside its protective tube (Photo: C. Huerta)

PUNTA CATIUS. THE CATHEDRAL ROCKS

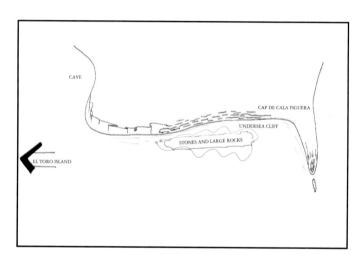

Technique:	medium
Average depth:	20 metres
Maximum depth:	32 metres
Duration:	40 minutes
Difficulties:	weather changes, anchoring and drift nets
Recommended season:	winter-spring

If the great dunes of the Teneré desert in Africa are called "cathedral dunes", at Punta Catius we can talk about "cathedral rocks".

Punta Catius is situated between the cape of Cala Figuera and the El Toro island. The cape of Cala Figuera closes the bay of Palma on the west, and the Cap Blanc closes it on the east.

It is necessary to have a boat to do this dive.

The nearest port is Port Adriano, at about six kilometres to the west, and the nearest place to launch a boat from a trailer into the sea is the cove of Portals Vells, at 2,5 kilometres to the east. At Port Adriano there is the Unidad Costa Norte diving centre, as well as a petrol station and other useful services.

Punta Catius is an easy dive. The whole area is suitable for scuba diving, from the Punta up until very near the cape of Cala Figuera, but you will find that the best dive is if you anchor 20 metres away from the cliff and 150 metres to the east of Punta Catius.

The sea floor is full of large rocks filled with cavities and bends where you find groupers at only a few metres of depth.

The area is suitable both for beginner and advan-

Rare specimen of John dory (*Zeus faber*), a very occasional encounter for divers (Photo: C. Huerta)

ced divers, but you must be specially careful with the nets that have fallen to the bottom and are caught on some of the rocks, and with the enormous amount of hooks and fishing lines that the fishermen of the coast leave on the "cathedral rocks".

Depending on the day and on the time of the year, you will find large white breams, groupers and brown meagres, or you may even see one or two John dories and triggerfish, but most of all, you will enjoy the overpowering view of the enormous underwater rocks, which look as if they had fallen from the cliff.

At the bottom you shall also see a large number of lines, wires, nets and rocks which are quite appropriate to lose your anchor for ever. It is important to check the anchor before rising up to the surface, and to fold it if at all possible to avoid getting it caught between the rocks.

Remember that this is an area of possible currents and sudden changes in the sea conditions.

During the summer months, the thermal wind from the area, called "embat" in Majorca, causes changes in the sea in a very short time.

During the midday hours, the warming up of the earth causes the air in contact with it to rise, thus creating strong air currents from the sea towards the coast.

Despite the fact that the sea bottom in this area is suitable to "crawl" if there are sea currents, it is best to find out the strength of these before going out diving in the sea.

The coast is a cliff and it is impossible to get to land from the sea in case of an emergency.

A good dive, easy and not too dangerous, the depth is not too great and the marine life is abundant.

1. Brown meagres (*Sciaena umbra*) swimming along a group of two-banded breams (*Diplodus vulgaris*) (Photo: A. Alonso).
2. A group of groupers (*Epinephelus guaza*) playing around with a diver. In natural circumstances these fish are extremely curious about divers (Photo: A. Alonso). 3. The remains of a lost net (Photo: C. Huerta)

SA CALOBRA. MORRO DE SA VACA

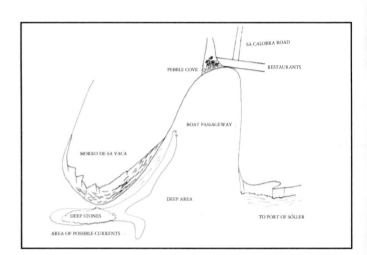

Technique:	medium, high
Average depth:	16 metres
Maximum depth:	30 metres
Duration:	60 minutes
Difficulties:	anchoring and currents
Recommended season:	summer, the summer thermal winds have little incidence on the north coast of Majorca.

At the Northeast of Majorca, the Serra de Tramuntana has produced a very steep and untamed coast. Enormous masses of rock look out to the sea, forming cliffs of hundreds of metres in height. These crags, that seem to defy the sea's strength, are as shocking below the water as they are on the outside.

If navigation in these waters is already a challenge, anchoring and diving around the area of Sa Calobra is an exciting adventure.

The enormous mound of Es Morro de sa Vaca closes the cove of Sa Calobra and its marine bottom is a combination of large rocks, holes and life, a lot of life.

Under the sea, the point of the Morro turns into a place where the abundant and strong water currents have allowed the proliferation of all sorts of species.

To get to the Morro it is necessary to go by sea with a boat. The nearest port is Sóller. In this town you can go to the diving centre which most often makes trips to Sa Calobra area and which best knows the area: the Octopus diving centre.

The distance from the port of Sóller to Sa Calobra is about ten nautical miles, so you will have to take into account the weather conditions before you decide to do this dive.

Impressive underwater landscape of the Majorcan north coast (Photo: C. Huerta)

Marbled electric ray (*Torpedo marmorata*). The Torpedinidae family have electric organs with which they stun their victims, small fish, by means of electric discharges (Photo: A. Torrens)

Once in Sa Calobra there are very few places to go for shelter with a boat. With a pneumatic dinghy though, you could go to Cala Tuent or the beach of Sa Calobra if necessary.

Anchor on the north side of the cove, near the vertex of the Morro de sa Vaca, and dive towards the point of the Morro. The depth reaches 40 metres at the centre of the cove. You must swim very close to the cliff, heading west, towards the cape.

Just below the Morro de sa Vaca you dive among large rocks, it is not very deep and it is not necessary to go any deeper to observe the characteristic species of these waters.

Below the Morro you may see gigantic dentexes, groupers and barracudas in small groups of three or four individuals.

At more depth –remember that you could go down to 40 metres– you can find yellow sea whips and some fish species that are typical of the coral reefs. The sardinie coral has already disappeared; however, its environment is still present in this place and many are the micro-organisms of all sorts that, since there is no coral, fall prey to sponges and corallines.

Around all this area, on the sand banks at the bottom of the water, you can observe blonde rays and marbled electric rays, specially during the winter.

Some fortunate divers have been able to see bluefin tuna fish, mostly during the summer, when, after their migration to the waters of the gulf of León, they go back to the Atlantic sea swimming parallel to the north coast of Majorca. The bluefin tuna fish has been swimming past these waters for millions of years and sometimes it can be seen very near the coast.

Yellow sea-whip (*Eunicella verrucosa*). It is found on the walls of dark rocks and on coral sea floors, mainly in the north, and it is particularly abundant in the area of Formentor (Photo: J. Serra)

PUNTA GALINDA. SUNKEN WRECK AT 37 METRES

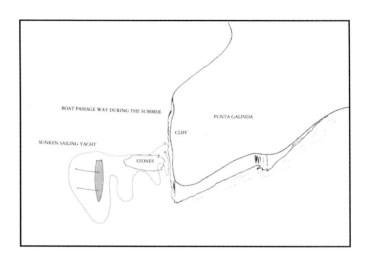

Technique:	medium high
Average depth:	30 metres
Maximum depth:	37 metres
Duration:	40 minutes
Difficulties:	depth, boats, sea conditions and sunken wreck
Recommended season:	spring-summer

Punta Galinda is at the south edge of the Sant Elm cove, and it has the Dragonera islet right in front. Sant Elm is the nearest port to Dragonera; the port of Andratx is not far either. A boat can be launched into the water from any of these ports.

The sunken wreck in Punta Galinda is at 37 metres of depth, it lies on the sand and it is in a very good condition. The wreck is an 18 metre long sailing yacht with 2 masts.

This sunken boat lies on its side, in a nearly upright position. It is near the coast, very few metres away from the point and from the cliff of Punta Galinda.

Going out on a boat from Sant Elm or the port of Andratx, you anchor 20 metres away from the point's cliff, over the coordinates l 39-33,9 N and L 002-20,8 E.

The anchor will touch the bottom at 24 metres of depth approximately. You must check the current and that the anchor is not moving along the bottom: you do not want your boat to end up being the second wreck in the area.

Anchoring at the specified coordinates, descend along the anchor line about 20 metres.

Dive along the natural decline of the sea bottom, heading away from the coast, approximately towards the south.

There is a long net caught between the rocks at about 28 metres of depth. It still continues its predatory work and it is a deadly trap for the fauna around the area.

After the area where the net is, diving towards the open sea and getting further away from the coast, you swim over a large sandbank at about 35 metres of depth.

You can see the sunken sailing yacht a few metres into the sandbank. Visibility is usually good, despite the fact that the starboard side of the wreck is at 37 metres of depth. The glass inside the boat's cabin is still intact, and the spars and the deck are in good condition. You have to move around the starboard side to notice the great hole in it.

You can enter the cabin through the stern, and you can reach the masts with the rig (being very careful with the cables and lines).

Taking into account the depth, you start the way back diving towards the coast, ascending gradually to eliminate nitrogen.

During the way back to the boat, the stones and rocks that seem to have fallen from the cliff in Punta Galinda can be observed in detail.

Using the anchor line you ascend gradually, bearing in mind the possible need for decompression. You must make safety stops and you must reach the surface near the boat, because there is usually an intense marine traffic during the summer.

Peyssonnelia squamaria. The red seaweeds are marine plants that live in poorly illuminated areas. You can find them at considerable depths and near the surface, although only on sombre walls and at the entrance of caverns. Inside the cells of many red seaweeds there are calcareous infiltrations, and these can be so abundant that the plant acquires a hardness similar to that of corals. (Photo: C. Huerta)

Sunken shipwrecks have a special appeal for divers, although they can turn out to be dangerous if they are not known or if they are explored without sufficient experience (Photo: J. Serra).

CORBERANA ISLAND. THE UNDERWATER BRIDGE

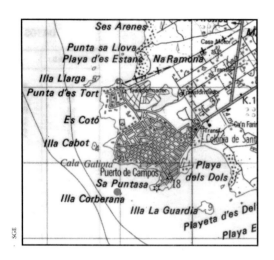

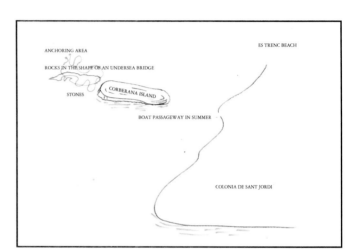

Technique:	low, medium
Average depth:	20 metres
Maximum depth:	26 metres
Duration:	50 minutes
Difficulties:	changes in the sea conditions, currents and anchoring
Recommended season:	spring

Corberana island is only a few hundreds of metres away from Colònia de Sant Jordi, in the south end of Majorca, very near the superb beach of Es Trenc.

As you go out of the Colònia de Sant Jordi's port, you head towards Sa Puntassa. Half a mile from Sa Puntassa is the island of Corberana, south of Colònia de San Jordi and east of the port. In the Colònia de Sant Jordi's port there is a public slipway and a petrol station.

You can look for an anchoring spot at the east of the islet, following its main axis, at about 250 metres from its southeast end. The ideal spot for anchoring is over the coordinates: 1 39-18,75 N

and L 002-59,17 E.

Anchoring is not always easy in this area, because of the changes in the sea conditions, particularly during the summer months.

The charts indicate between 10 and 20 metres of depth. Over the coordinates mentioned above you find an area of large rocks and stones that form tunnels and bridges of fanciful shapes and look as if they had been built by man.

The "underwater bridge", has really curious shapes, it is at about 19 metres of depth and it is the end of a rocky barrier that starts at the southeast end of the Corberana island.

From the anchoring line you descend 20

metres approximately and you head towards the underwater bridge. This formation is a group of large rocks in the shape of a bridge with various arches through which two or three divers can swim at the same time.

Inside the bridge's holes live some small groupers and other characteristic species of rocks and caves.

You start the dive at the bridge and dive heading northeast towards the island. You find arches and cavities that form an extraordinary landscape. The ceiling of these caverns is covered with corals and sponges, and since the light is not sufficient, the flashlight and the torch are essential to appreciate their brilliant colours.

You start the way back over the same route, heading southwest. You do it at less depth, swimming over the rocks.

If you return swimming at less depth you shall be able to avoid the required decompression stops.

Small grouper (*Epinephelus guaza*) in its hiding place surrounded by branches of false coral (*Myriapora truncata*). Unlike Sardinie coral, the false coral has no commercial value because it looses its colour a few days after it is taken out of the water (Photo: A. Alonso)

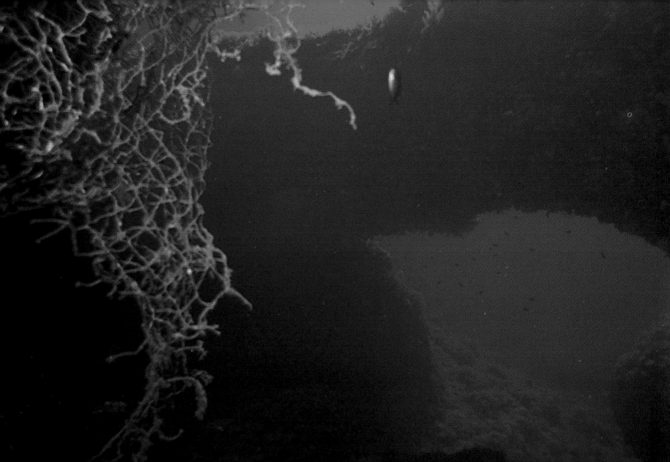

1. Undersea landscape at Corberana island. 2. Flying gunard (*Dactylopterus volitans*) trapped in a fishing net. The nets that get lost after storms or because they hit a rock continue their useless destructive toil, trapping fish, crustaceans and molluscs which will in turn become bait for new victims (Photo: A. Alonso).

EL TORO ISLAND. WEST SIDE

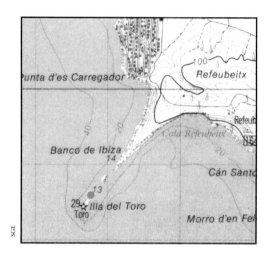

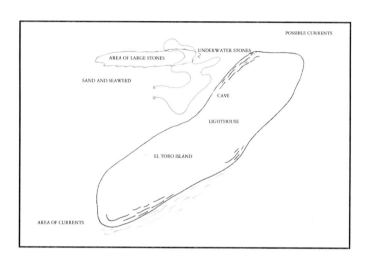

Technique:	low, medium
Average depth:	20 metres
Maximum depth:	38 metres
Duration:	50 minutes
Difficulties:	strong currents and heavy maritime traffic
Recommended season:	spring-autumn

This is a medium level dive, however, any person can do it because it allows beginners to explore the north side of the islet without going too deep, and it also invites the experts to go lower than 30 metres and only a few metres away from the rocky wall of the island.

El Toro is an islet that lies southwest of Majorca, near the bay of Palma, between Portals Vells and Santa Ponça.

It is necessary to use a boat to get to the islet. El Toro is an ideal place for non-professional diving and there are a number of diving centres that organise dives in these waters, particularly Unidad Costa Norte, Escuba Palma and Calumet.

The nearest port is Port Adriano, which is practically in line with El Toro island.

Coming out of Port Adriano you take a southern direction and, approximately one and a half mile away is El Toro island. It is unmistakable, it is the prolongation of a long and slender cape called Banc d'Eivissa. On the islet of El Toro there is a lighthouse at 30 metres of height. You must be aware that between the Banc d'Eivissa and El Toro island there are some passage ways for boats and that the depth is a maximum of 14 metres, therefore it is not convenient to anchor in the channel, and even less so to go diving in it.

1. Cardinal fish (*Apogon imberbis*) and a large scaled scorpion fish (*Scorpaena scrofa*). The orange colouration of the cardinal fish makes them specially attractive for undersea photographers. 2. An octopus (*Octopus vulgaris*) observing from its hideaway. Octopuses mate at the end of the summer and spawn hundreds of thousands of eggs (Photos: A. Alonso)

Once there, you anchor on the west side of the islet (if the sea conditions make anchoring on the east side more suitable, that is a different dive, and it is described in another chapter).

You drop the anchor roughly about half way along the cliff's wall, 20 metres away from the coast. The anchor will touch the bottom at 30 metres of depth, and you must let go a lot of line to avoid dragging on the bottom and swinging at anchor.

To start the dive you first go down to the maximum depth, which is 38 metres. If some of the members of the group have a lower level of technique, you can swim around the islet's coast, depending on the direction of the current, and always starting to swim against the direction of the current.

The deepest area is full of life and it is surprising because it still has the remains of various vessels that are over 2,000 years old. You can still see bits of amphorae and vessels in these waters. Remember that whoever dives in this area in the future will also want to see these remains and that the law prohibits the plundering of sunken shipwrecks.

On the west wall of the island there is a small cave that hides goldcrests and hermit crabs, and it can be visited quite safely. Near the cave there is a "bar" that goes down to 35 metres and it is normally inhabited by morays and a few conger eels.

Some barracudas, tunas, dolphins and blue sharks have been seen in the waters near El Toro. It is normal to easily see dentexes and large sea basses.

El Toro is without a doubt one of the favourite areas for many non-professional divers, among other reasons because no matter how often it is visited, it always looks different.

Barracudas (*Sphyraena sphyraena*) (Photo: C. Huerta)

CALA SANTANYÍ. THE CAVES

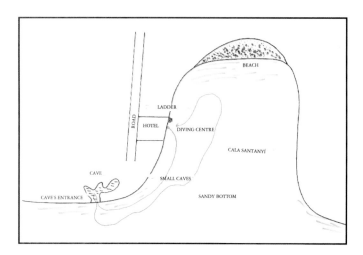

Technique:	medium
Average depth:	12 metres
Maximum depth:	16 metres
Duration:	50 minutes
Difficulties:	the usual difficulties of caves
Recommended season:	the low depth and the access from land make this dive suitable for the winter

There are a number of possibilities for diving in Cala Santanyí; one of them is exploring the caves in the south side.

The caves of Cala Santanyí are not very difficult nor dangerous, they are full of the characteristic species of large undersea caves and they end in vaults with open and breathable ceilings.

You start the dive at the Albatros diving centre, where it is advisable to get some details and information about the sea conditions and the state of the caves. At this diving centre, below the Pinos playa hotel, in Cala Santanyí itself, you can hire diving equipment or refill your air cylinders.

At the cove there is a small ladder to get into the water, you will use it when you start and to come out after the dive.

After going down the steps you descend around 5 metres into a water which is normally clean and crystal clear, and you dive towards the entrance of the cove, following the direction of the small cliff over which the Pinos Playa hotel is built.

Maintain the sandy area of the cove to your left and the cliff's rocks to your right.

The depth increases gradually, but it does not reach 15 metres at any point.

Just at the end of the cove, below the point of the small cape that encloses Cala Santanyí, you will find, at more or less 14 metres of depth, the entrance to the caves.

Naturally, it is quite necessary to take torches or flashlights. Make sure to take sufficient lights, because getting out of the dark cave with no light can be very difficult.

The entrance is not easily found because it is always in the dark. The cave must be explored very carefully, and unless you are quite experienced, it is much better to go with somebody who knows it, such as a guide from the Albatros club.

The caves are not deep enough to get lost inside them, but it is preferable to go in very cautiously and checking the orientation, even with a safety line. They are not dangerous caves, but there are numerous cavities and twists and turns that could confuse those less experienced in cave diving.

Near the entrance of the caves, if you are not too rackety, you will be able to see a few very large brown meagres and some solitary groupers.

After exploring the main cave you will see the brightness of the final vault, where you can emerge to the surface.

Darkness is total except for the light of the torches and flashlights. Emerging to the surface inside the vault has to be done carefully, feeling the ceiling first with one hand and keeping the arm vertical, to check that there are no rocks before putting your heads out of the water.

Inside the vault, which is the size of a large room, you can take out your regulator and breathe the air easily, at more or less 30 or 40 metres from the entrance to the cave.

Brown meagres (*Sciaena umbra*) suffer the proliferation of small parasite crustaceans that can weaken them to death. (Photo: A. Alonso)

1. Striped red mullet (*Mullus surmuletus*). It feeds from small molluscs, crustaceans and worms. (Photo: A. Alonso). 2. Red octopus of nocturnal habits. 3. Starfish (*Ophidiaster ophidianus*). Starfish are highly voracious carnivore animals that feed on bivalves and gastropods which they suction with their stomach, which they can pull out of their bodies (Photo: A. Alonso). 4. Snakelocks anemone (*Anemonia sulcata*). It sometimes lives very near the surface (Photo: C. Huerta)

MALGRATS ISLANDS. THE CLIFF

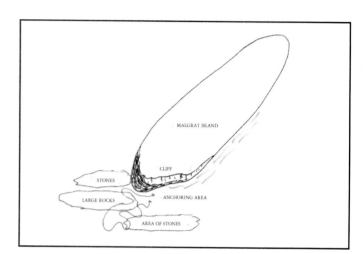

Technique:	high
Average depth:	26 metres
Maximum depth:	40 metres
Duration:	60 minutes
Difficulties:	maritime traffic
Recommended season:	spring and autumn, when we may find the pelagic species coming close to the coast to spawn.

In the submerged extension of the Malgrats islands, near Port Adriano, between Santa Ponça and El Toro, there is a huge underwater cliff that reaches 40 metres in steep descent.

The Malgrats islands seem to extend under the sea towards the southwest, advancing into the depths and turning into a real nursery of all sorts of species.

The nearest port from the islands is Santa Ponça and the nearest diving centre is Escuba Palma, which organises dives around the Malgrats islands. The whole area between El Toro island and the Malgrats islands is in the process of

becoming (that is the wish of all the non-professional divers) a marine reserve area, which would confirm it as one of the most suitable places for scuba diving in Majorca, together with the island of Cabrera.

The marine life is very abundant around all this part of the south coast of Majorca, but, according to the experts, the over-exploitation of the sea by professional and non-professional fishing has reduced the Malgrats islands' capacity to provide and develop its own fauna.

The Malgrats islets are a passage and settling area for many species, and in these waters it is

Moruna. Labyrinth-like fishing net (Photo: A. Alonso)

1. *Caulerpa prolifera*. Common seaweed in ports over sandy sea floors; not to be confused with the so-called "killer seaweed", *Caulerpa taxifolia* (Photo: C. Huerta). 2. Barracuda (*Sphyraena sphyraena*) trapped in a net (Photo: A. Alonso). 3. Conger eel (*Conger conger*). A mighty predator of twilight time habits, it can reach two metres of length and 50 kilos of weight (Photo: A. Alonso)

possible to observe a great number of living creatures in the reproductive stage at any time of the year. The microplancton and the moderate current complete the reproductive and food cycles, which makes the Malgrats a paradise for scuba diving and the conservation of nature.

The most suitable part of the islands for non-professional diving is at the far end of the main islet.

Going out on a boat from any of the nearby ports, it is very easy to find the anchoring spot, just at the end of the point of the islet, 30 metres away from the steep coast.

You have to try to anchor over some rocks that are very near the cliff, because the depth exceeds 40 metres if you go more than 50 metres away from the coast.

You start the dive descending along the anchor's line, and checking that the anchor is all right. The dive has to be done descending directly to the bottom of the stunning cliff, that falls from 12 to about 35 or 40 metres. You can practically descend vertically down until the underwater cliff reaches the sandy bottom. At the end of the cliff it looks as if there are no more rocks, but if you continue moving towards the undersea plane, after about 200 metres you get to another group of rocks. This rocky area, quite distant from the undersea cliff, is at about 40 metres of depth, and inside its cracks and holes there hide enormous conger and moray eels. From this point you must start the return journey, ascending slowly towards the point of the Malgrats' main islet, as if "climbing" the submerged rocks.

ES TRENC BEACH. BAIX DEL TENC

Technique:	low
Average depth	16 metres
Maximum depth:	19 metres
Duration:	50 minutes
Difficulties:	boat traffic
Recommended season:	spring

Opposite the beach of Es Trenc there is an area which is suitable for non-professional diving, but it is imperative to be very careful with the maritime traffic, specially during the summer, because in this area it is very busy.

The Baix is in front of Es Trenc, but at enough distance to make it impossible to start the dive from land. It is necessary to have a boat, preferably one equipped with a GPS and an echo sounder to find the right place, because fixing one's position with alignments is quite difficult.

The coordinates of the exact spot where you are heading to are: l 39-19,75 N and L 002-58,46 E.

Once you get to the diving area, it is conve-nient to find the anchoring place with an echo sounder. One of the centres that dives often in this area is Isurus Subaquatic, from Palma, and it performs practice dives and dives for beginners.

The sea floor in El Baix de Es Trenc is rocky, full of stones and considerably sized holes. There is a gallery which is outstanding because it looks like a man made tunnel. This tunnel is ideal for beginners to practice cave diving, it is about 18 metres long and quite narrow.

Apart from this tunnel in Baix del Trenc, there is also a huge stone arch and many cracks between the large rocks that make the dive interesting.

There are some times of the year when it is unusual to see any large fish around this area, but during some months you can frequently see gilthead breams, amber Jacks, groupers and meagres, as well as considerably sized large scaled scorpion fish.

The dive is done vertically down and the maximum depth that you are going to reach is 19 metres. One of the possibilities is to describe a large circle around the boat, exploring the stones and the cracks on the sea floor. It is necessary to use a flashlight or torch. It can also be a very good dive to do by night.

You must be aware at all times of the movement of speed boats and all sorts of sailing yachts around here; these last ones cannot be heard from under the water and they can therefore give you, in the best of cases, a shock as you ascend to the surface.

The difficulty of this dive is basically locating the right diving spot in the first place. This is only possible with the aid of electronic means or by having a very good knowledge of the area. Secondly, you must not forget the already mentioned maritime traffic risk.

At the anchoring place it is not unusual to find people in dinghies fishing with bait and some underwater fishermen trawling the bottom.

It is possible to get to Baix del Trenc in just a few minutes with a small boat, starting from the nearby ports of S'Estanyol or Sa Ràpita, and also from the Colònia de Sant Jordi.

As well as the usual fish from the area you will also be able to observe beadlets, various anemone species, sea cucumbers, madrepores and one or two peltodoris.

The Isurus II in S'Estanyol waters. Non-professional diving tourism has proliferated in the last few years in Majorca (Photo: J. Poyatos)

1. Heading towards Baix del Trenc (Photo: J. Poyatos). 2. Amber Jacks (*Seriola dumerili*). Habitual visitor of the high sea-weeds during the summer months. (Photo: A. Torrens)

CALA D'OR. NA SECA

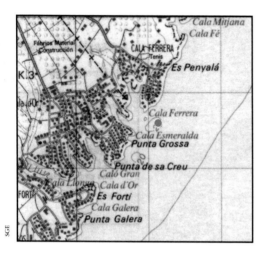

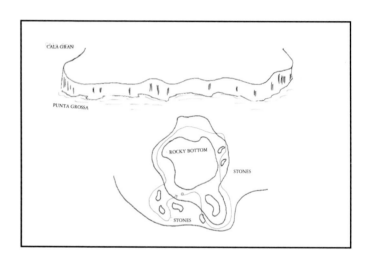

Technique:	medium
Average depth:	20 metres
Maximum depth:	30 metres
Duration:	40 minutes
Difficulties:	the frequent passage of boats
Recommended season:	summer

Opposite the well known tourist development of Cala d'Or, between Cala Gran and Cala Ferrera, there is an undersea rocky mound at about 20 metres of depth. This unusual formation is approximately 180 metres away from the coast.

Funnily, the fauna around this undersea mound is very trusting and unafraid, fish such as groupers and other species allow the divers to get really close to them without taking too many precautions. The affluence of dozens of respectful subaquatic tourists to this area has made the fish in Na Seca very confident, and they swim comfortably and fearlessly among their visitors.

It is easy to locate this undersea mound,

because, and specially during the summer, it is perfectly visible from the surface of the water when you go over it in a boat.

You anchor over the large undersea rock and start the underwater journey describing a long circle around Na Seca.

In this area, which is overpopulated by the characteristic Mediterranean fauna, you can explore one place or another according to the movements of the living creatures that you might observe among the rocks and cavities.

On the north side of the large undersea mound you find exuberant life, and sometimes, curious groupers that look out from their holes to see the divers swim by.

122

1-2. Octopuses and groupers are the two most characteristic species of the Mediterranean sea (Photos: A. Torrens)

1. Close-up of a rainbow (*Coris julis*). When it feels threatened it buries itself in the sand with a hearty tail swipe; acting the same way at dusk, to sleep, and when the water temperature drops below 14°C. (Photo: C. Huerta). 2. Safety stops returning to the surface (Photo: C. Huerta). 3. Two-banded bream (*Diplodus vulgaris*). They live in large groups and have characteristic dark marks (Photo: C. Huerta)

It is also possible to observe schools of fairly sized barracudas which appear to feel curious about the bubbles that the visitors exhale through their strange tubes. Remember that the barracudas usually stay at a reasonable distance from the divers, swimming in concentric circles around them. If you remain nearly motionless and without making any sudden movements, they may start to describe smaller and smaller circles around you, until they get really close.

North-east from Na Seca you will see a rock that forms a pointed crest that drops when it gets to the deepest area. At the foot of the crest there are numerous small caves inhabited by small crustaceans and colourful goldcrests, and on the east slope of the main rocky mound there is a cave which is larger than the rest and it is visited very regularly by divers from the nearest diving centres, because it is indeed teeming with life.

After you have circled around the mound, you start the way back to the boat, checking first that you do not need to make any decompression stops. Some *sparidae* will be swimming next to you, in fact they will have accompanied you during the whole dive around the beautiful underwater rock of Na Seca.

SA FORADADA. ES CUCÓ

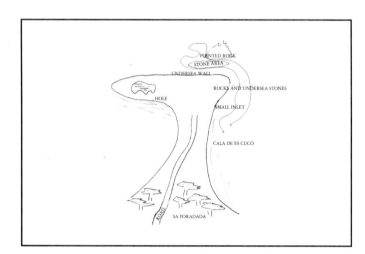

Technique:	medium, high
Average depth:	20 metres
Maximum depth:	34 metres
Duration:	50 minutes
Difficulties:	the depth and currents
Recommended season:	summer

In the Tramuntana mountains, between the port of Sóller and the port of Valldemossa, is the very curious rocky formation known as Sa Foradada. It is a cape that stretches towards the sea and that after a curve towards the south it appears like a wall with a large hole.

The west side of Majorca is known as the area of the Tramuntana mountains, and it is famous for being inhospitable because of its characteristic weather and the sea conditions. The truth is that, during most part of the year, the steep west coast is calmer than the flat east part of the island.

The "January calms" in Majorca are well-known, they are periods of time when the sun shines and there is practically no wind. These January calms allow the diver to enjoy a dive in Sa Foradada in very calm and crystal clear waters.

The proliferation of marine life in this part of the coast is enormous, but this is not necessarily because of any special biological conditions, but because of the orographic difficulties for practising underwater fishing, either professional or non-professional.

To get to Sa Foradada it is necessary to do so by boat; the nearest port is the port of Sóller. There you will find a public slipway and a petrol station, as well as all the other typical services of any city. The diving centre that does most dives around Sa Foradada is the Octopus diving centre, from the port of Sóller. At this centre they have a boat which is adequate to confront the possible weather changes and the more or less lengthy crossings that are made in this coast.

Sa Foradada offers a number of different and interesting dives; one of them, which can be done if the sea and anchoring conditions allow it, is the one known as "Es Cucó".

For this dive, you drop the anchor at approximately 12 metres of depth, on the north side of the great cape of Sa Foradada, at the opposite end of the hole.

This area is adequate for anchoring when the wind and the sea are from the south, then the boat will be sheltered. If however, the wind and the sea are from the north, you can explore the area that is just under the hole.

You start the dive heading towards the west, following the natural curve of the Foradada's rocky outcrop. You border the northeast side of the great crag, but without reaching the area beneath the hole.

Just as you turn the northeast point, diving at 20 metres of depth, you find a group of large and pointy rocks that are full of holes and that reach down to 34 metres of depth.

The large rocks, that look as if they had fallen off the wall of Sa Foradada, are absolutely full of groupers, corvachos and enormous greater forkbeards that wander around the dark areas of the holes.

The flashlight is quite necessary, particularly if you are diving during the morning, when the diving area is on the shady side of Sa Foradada.

Among the rocks at the bottom there is an enormous pointed rock that stands out and ends in a group of stones that hide many fish of all kinds. Species like anthias (or swallowtail sea perch), which are rare in other parts of Majorca, can be seen here.

1-2 The sea bottom at Es Trenc is magnificent because of the number of caves and canopies that form at the base. (Photos: C. Huerta). 3. Brown wrasse (*Labrus merula*). One of the largest Labridae, it is usually seen hiding under the rocks and always alone (Photo: C. Huerta). 4. The greater forkbeard (*Phycis phycis*) lives at great depths, under large rocks and inside caves (Photo: A. Torrens).

PORT DE SÓLLER. COVA DES PINTOR

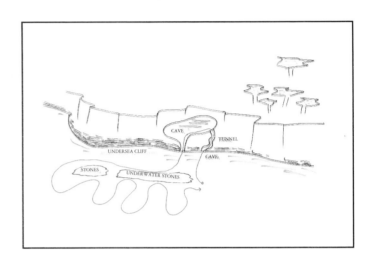

Technique:	medium
Average depth:	16 metres
Maximum depth:	24 metres
Duration:	60 minutes
Difficulties:	those of caves and currents
Recommended season:	spring and summer

The dive to Sa Cova des Pintor (the painter's cave) and around its entrance is a required experience when diving in Majorca.

The cave's special shape and the rocks near its entrance are a perfect setting for non-professional diving.

The diving area has to be reached by boat. It is advisable to explore the cave with somebody who knows the place well. The safest thing to do is to go to the Octopus diving centre at the port of Sóller, where there are experienced divers who know the cave and its conditions.

From the port of Sóller you head towards the south and go around Cap Gros, to anchor in front of the painter's cave, only one mile away more or less from the port.

The cave is easily identified because it has an enormous entrance by land. At the base of the cave there are some man-made cement steps said to have been built by the painter who once lived there. It may be possible that this painter existed, but according to the town's inhabitants, the steps and the cave had always been used by local smugglers during the postwar years.

Even from land, the cave deserves an exploration by foot, because it is quite large and spectacular.

The underwater cave, which is under the presu-

Cons

med painter's "home", has an entrance at 13 metres of depth and it ascends to the surface through a sort of chimney, finally joining the exterior cave.

You cannot get lost inside the underwater cave, but you must be aware that it ascends nearly 14 metres, therefore the buoyancy control problems that some beginners may experience can cause them to get stuck to the ceiling.

The remains of old sacks, empty bottles, old packaging and other characteristic objects from the postwar's smuggling years have been found near the exterior entrance of the painter's cave.

At the north of the cave's underwater entrance, about ten metres away from it, there are a group of large rocks which, at 20 metres of depth, are teeming with life.

Barracudas, dentexes, sea basses, gilthead breams, large white breams and all kinds of saupes and two-banded breams meander in groups of hundreds, or even thousands, among the rocks of this very special place.

You can start this dive by exploring the cave, and then having a look around the rocks at the entrance.

If the sea conditions allow for it, it is worthwhile to explore the cave by foot, from land. It is possible to approach a boat to the cement stairs that indicate the entrance.

Try to be environmentally friendly, picking up the rubbish that the sea may have washed onto the cave. And remember that apart from the beauty of the underwater and land cave, there are also the rocks at the entrance that are full of life.

131

BS

132

Previous page, above: Two-banded bream (*Diplodus vulgaris*) (Photo: A. Alonso). Over these lines: the painter's cave, place known in Sóller for serving during the post-war years as a hide for smugglers (Photo: J. Poyatos)

FORMENTOR. CAP CATALUNYA, LOBSTERS AND SEA WHIPS

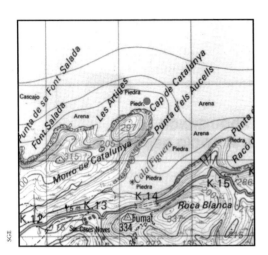

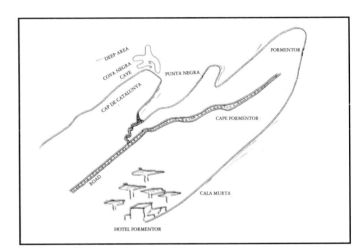

Technique:	medium, high
Average depth:	26 metres
Maximum depth:	30 metres
Duration:	60 minutes
Difficulties:	to get there by boat
Recommended season:	summer

The so-called Morro de Catalunya is a lateral extension of the cape of Formentor that points towards the Iberian Peninsula. It is the portion of land of Majorca closest to Tarragona.

The nearest place from the Cap de Catalunya to launch a small boat into the water is Port de Pollença. From this port you have to go to the cape of Formentor and further, which is certainly not an easy task, because there are nearly 12 miles of route, and you have to go around the cape, where the sea is not usually very easy. After the cape of Formentor you head southwest.

There are two nautical miles from the Formentor lighthouse to the cape of Catalunya, a rocky mass of nearly 300 metres of height that falls straight down to the sea. The rock of the Morro de Catalunya continues under the sea level and reaches 60 metres of depth.

You anchor under the cape of Catalunya, a few metres away from the cliff, at the west end of the cape, but without going further than the cape.

All the area that lies under the cape is a good diving area to observe lobsters and yellow sea whips.

It is much better to do this dive during a summer afternoon, that is when the sun light will make things easier and prevent any sudden weather changes because of thermal changes.

Remember that it is impossible to hold on to the coast and that the nearest place to go for shelter is Cala Figuera, southwest from the cape of Catalunya. You can get to Cala Figuera by car with a four wheel drive vehicle, however, it would be very difficult to transport a boat down the track; but it can serve as a shelter in case of an emergency.

The sea bottom at Cap de Catalunya rapidly descends to 40 metres, it has to be explored very carefully, descending more or less according to your experience and to the sea conditions.

Without going down more than 30 metres deep you will find rocks with cracks where, mostly during summer and spring, you may see lobsters, meagres, large scaled scorpion fish and yellow sea whips.

The yellow sea whip is an animal which has the shape of a vertical stick and the appearance of a plant. It has a hard feel to the touch, it feeds by filtering the water that goes through its polyps and it lives at depths of up to 20 metres. Around the Formentor area, specially the cape of Catalunya, is where it can be seen more profusely. At depths of more than 40 metres, also between the cape of Catalunya and the Formentor lighthouse, it is possible to see the rare red sea whip, very abundant in the past but sadly exhausted today and affected a great deal by pollution.

Lobsters are abundant around the cape, they look out from their cracks to observe the divers; it is very easy to touch them or even pick them up, but that is really unnecessary and they can get hurt if you do try to touch them.

The many photographs you can take of the lobsters, of the several caves in the undersea cliff, of the sea whips and the rocks that have fallen from the Morro de Catalunya, all justify doing this relatively difficult dive.

The rock blenny (*Parablennius gattorugine*) known also as tompot blenny, is a very bad swimmer and only budges a few metres when it feels threatened (Photo: C. Huerta).

Spectacular multicolour violescent sea-whip (*Aparamunicea chamaleon*). This sea-whip is very rare in the Balearic crystal clear waters, it can only be seen at great depths and at the foot of cliffs that guard them from excessive light (Photo: A. Torrens).

CAP DES LLAMP. DIVING PARALLEL TO THE GREAT WALL

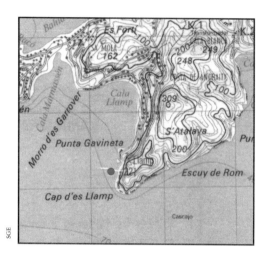

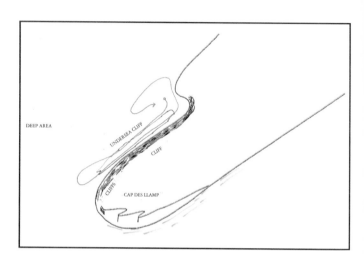

Technique:	medium
Average depth:	18 metres
Maximum depth:	24 metres
Duration:	50 minutes
Difficulties:	possible currents
Recommended season:	spring

The Cap des Llamp is near the port of Andratx, soon after going around the cape of Sa Mola, heading towards Santa Ponça. It is a rocky cape crowned by the so-called Cap des Llamp (cape of the lightning), of 221 metres of height. You must get to Cap des Llamp by boat from the port of Andratx, Sant Elm, or Port Adriano.

At the Port of Andratx, under the bridge of the Saluet torrent, there is a public slipway where you can launch a small boat into the water.

There is also a petrol station and a diving cen-

tre, the Aquamarine, at the Port of Andratx, as well as the other usual services of any marina and fishing port.

At the Aquamarine diving centre there are renting facilities for equipment, and the staff offers detailed information about the diving area and the sea conditions.

Coming out of the port of Andratx you head southwest until you go around de Cap de Sa Mola. The next cape, heading east, is the Cap des Llamp.

1. Explosion of life and colour. 2. Spiny lobster (*Palinurus vulgaris*). Lobsters perform long migrations walking at great depth over the sandy sea floor (Photo: C. Huerta).

Over these lines: the dive at these depths requires a lot of experience and training. (Photo: A. Torrens). Next page, below: Anglerfish (*Lophius piscatorius*). One of the most outstanding examples of camouflage. They also have a curious predatory strategy: when they see a small fish, they attract its attention with an undulating movement of the dermic lobe that they have at the end of their dorsal radius, which acts as a bait; when the prey gets close enough, the anglerfish engulfs it with an extraordinarily swift movement (Photo: C. Huerta).

You anchor between Punta Gavineta and the point of the cape, on the west side of the Cap des Llamp, not very far from a very small cove.

Only 20 metres away from the steep coast, the depth is of more or less 18 metres.

Descending along the anchor line you will find a rocky bottom and the vertical wall of the Cap des Llamp's cliff that continues under the sea. The sight of this cliff under the water is quite impressive.

You dive against the current, which is frequent in this area during some months of the year, moving along the cliff's underwater wall.

The marine fauna is not particularly abundant, but visibility is usually very good and the effect of the cliff and the divers "overflying" the deepness is well worth it.

The return has to be done with enough margin on the manometer, taking into account the currents and the possible need for decompression stops.

At the end of the cape, just at the point of the Cap des Llamp, there is a group of stones where it is not unusual to find groupers of a respectable size.

This is a suitable dive to do with a group of people or with inexperienced divers who want to gradually get used to the depths and the sensations that rocks and vertical walls give.

The rocky area, which is practically a completely different dive, has to de done with somewhat more experience than the wall, and being aware of the currents and the sea conditions, apart from making sure that the anchor is holding correctly.

CALA RATJADA. COVA DES COLOMS AND CALA DES VELL MARÍ

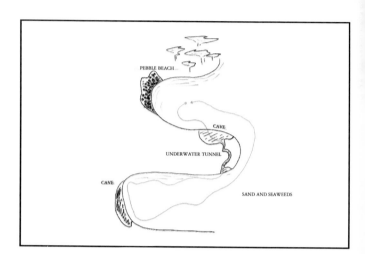

Technique:	medium
Average depth:	10 metres
Maximum depth:	18 metres
Duration:	70 minutes
Difficulties:	the narrow gallery
Recommended season:	winter and spring

This is an easy dive. It can start from land and it is interesting because of the changing sea floor and because there are caves and underwater galleries to explore.

The Cova des Coloms (cave of the pigeons) and the Cala des Vell Marí (cove of the Mediterranean seal) are a diving area suitable for beginners and to do an easy dive; this area is between Cala Ratjada and the Costa des Pins, northeast of Majorca.

If you start the dive from a small boat, you can launch it into the water from the public slipway at Cala Ratjada. From there you head south, towards Cap Vermell. From land, you can get to the Cala des Vell Marí by car. When you get in the water, you dive towards the point of the cove, heading southeast. The entrance to the first of the underwater caves is visible from the Cala des Vell Marí, a pebble cove, because it is right there, and it has a gallery that goes to the next underwater cave, outside the Cala des Vell Marí.

If you have arrived by boat, you will anchor at the south part of the cove, near where the entrance of the large cave is.

1. Cova des Coloms (Photo: C. Huerta). 2. Jellyfish (*Pelagia noctiluca*) in front of a rock full of bryozoae and hexacoralliae (Photo: A. Alonso).

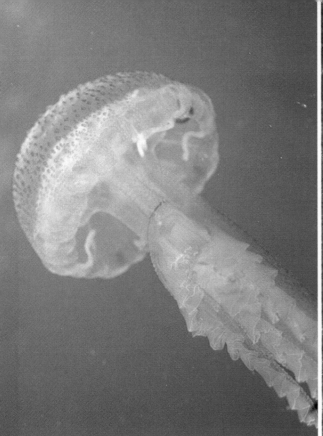

1. *Clathrina clathrus*, sponge (Photo: C. Huerta). 2. Long-snouted wrasse (*Symphodus rostratus*). Endemic species in the Mediterranean. 3. Small prawn (*Palaemon elegans*). During the day it hides in caves and cracks, coming out at night to look for food. 4. Close-up of a *Pelagia noctiluca*. 5. Common sting-ray (*Dasyatis pastinaca*). Its sting contains poison (Photos: A. Alonso).

You explore the first cave. It is quite large and it has a number of passages and concealed spaces where brown meagres and Cape town lobsters hide. There are also *Cerianthus* and curious mounds of sand at the bottom of the cave. These craters in the mud confirm the proliferation of nocturnal life. Hermit crabs, shells of all kinds and small shrimps move around inside de cave.

After exploring the large cave at the cove, move on to the second cave, going around the cliff on the south side. Following the rocky outcrop, just after getting out of the cove, you enter a new cave, with passages and a gallery that goes back to the first cave. This tunnel must not be explored unless there is somebody with you who knows these galleries, because even though they are not very difficult caves, the claustrophobic sensation can cause some inexperienced divers to get nervous.

The third cave, which is perfectly visible from the surface of the water, is called Cova des Coloms (the pigeons' cave). It is an area known to some fishermen who, with their cartridge shotguns, have practically exterminated the pigeons that had always nested there.

The tourist boats that organise excursions during the summer to this place get right inside the Cova des Coloms (beware in summer, as the water in the cave is shallow). From the diver's point of view, this cave is not very interesting, there is not much marine life in it and it does not have many ramifications; however, among the rocks at the entrance you will see, if you look carefully, solitary groupers, white breams, and one or two sporadic white crabs inside the abundant fan mussels. There are also some leaf shaped worms, cuttlefish and even one or two sea horses amid the seaweeds.

This dive is suitable for divers with a medium level of technique who want to experience the sensation of diving inside a cave.

CALA RATJADA. THE FARALLÓ DE CALA GAT ISLET

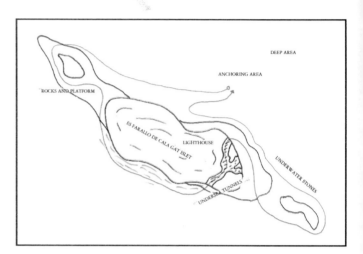

Technique:	low, medium
Average depth:	12 metres
Maximum depth:	18 metres
Duration:	60 minutes
Difficulties:	the busy maritime traffic
Recommended season:	spring and autumn

The Faralló dive cannot be missing in a book of non-professional diving in Majorca. This small islet represents an easy diving day and its sea bottom is surprisingly brimming with exuberant life, being as it is so close to a populated coast and to a port with a busy maritime traffic.

Es Faralló is a small islet opposite the port of Cala Ratjada. Its abundant marine life can be observed with no difficulty at all. This abundance of life is due probably to the constant currents that provide nutrients and thermal waters. It is a small islet that can be circled completely with no problems in one outing and in less than one hour.

You can launch a boat in the water from the public slipway at the Cala Ratjada port, then you have to head towards the east side of its entrance.

Following the course to Minorca, but only a hundred metres away from the port, you will see the unmistakable Faralló islet.

The anchor will go down approximately 20 metres, and you have to anchor according to the sea conditions. Try to stay to leeward, taking into

1. Faralló de Cala Gat (Photo: C. Huerta). 2. Amber Jack (*Seriola dumerili*). When they are adult they live alone and can reach one metre in length (Photo: A. Alonso)

Octopus (*Octopus vulgaris*). What looks like the head is really the powerful muscle that allows it to eject water at great pressure in order to propel it at great speed in the water (Photo: C. Huerta).

account the current, which can be strong and different to the direction of the wind.

Weather changes are not unusual in this part of Majorca, therefore it is advisable to find out in advance about the meteorological previsions, and to consult about the situation of the sea and the diving conditions at the Mero diving centre, in Cala Lliteres, not far from Cala Ratjada. At this centre they organise group outings to various sites around this area, which has many good diving possibilities.

The southeast side of Es Faralló de Cala Gat is the most interesting one, there the islet seems to be traversed by tunnels and galleries that make up suitable habitats for greater forkbeards, meagres, groupers, morays and all sorts of filtering organisms such as sea whips and false coral. Also, you might have some dentexes and other fish observing you from a cautious distance.

The whole of the southeast side of Es Faralló is fascinating for any diver; its galleries and holes are full of sea sponges and other organisms which are characteristic of places with regular currents. Near the rocks there are a large number of amber jacks, striped grey mullets, saddled breams and a few sea basses.

If the weather at sea is good and the temperature of the water is pleasant, you will enjoy an unforgettable and very colourful dive with exuberant marine life, and experience sensations of changing lights and shades.

Seeing the other members of the group moving through the caves and holes will make this fascinating diving experience even more attractive. This dive never fails to captivate. It is not a complicated one; the only concern is anchoring in this busy maritime traffic area, it has to be done with special precaution, particularly during the summer.

WEST DOCK. THE DOCK'S THREE CAVES

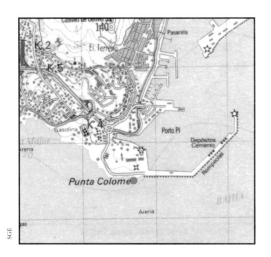

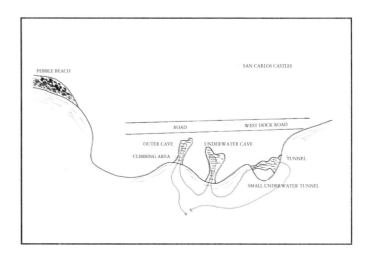

Technique:	medium
Average depth:	8 metres
Maximum depth:	16 metres
Duration:	40 minutes
Difficulties:	anchoring, maritime traffic and caves
Recommended season:	winter, on a day when the wind blows from the north, clearing the usually cloudy waters of the bay of Palma.

Palma's three caves are located between the palace of Marivent and the west dock. These are a group of cracks, caves and passages alongside the coast that cannot be classified as being difficult, in spite the fact that the current and the frequent maritime traffic, especially during the summer, forces divers to have special precautions during the dive.

The three caves have their entrance at about 12 metres of depth and in one of them there is an opening to a breathable vault.

The dive has to start from a boat; the nearest places to launch an inflatable dinghy into the water are the yacht club in Cala Nova or the Portitxol club.

Finding the entrances of the caves is not very difficult; however, it could be risky to explore them without an experienced person who knows them previously. The nearest diving centre is Calumet, below the Bonanza Hotel in Illetes. At Calumet they regularly organise outings to the dock's three caves.

The entrance to the first cave is at more or less 12 metres of depth, just below a small cliff where, mostly on Sundays, there are often people practising free climbing. The cave can be seen from the surface of the water, and you can anchor right in front of it.

1. Boarding at the Bonanza Hotel (Photo: J. Poyatos). 2. The greater forkbeard (*Phycis phycis*) lives practically in the darkness of deep caves (Photo: A. Alonso)

151

1. Close-up of a moray eel. 2. Triggerfish (*Balistes carolinensis*). It is a fish from tropical waters that reaches the Mediterranean and European coasts, carried by the gulf's current. 3. The dock's caves. 4. Congers are fish of nocturnal habits. Occasionally they get so dangerously close to the divers that these have to protect their face and hands (Photos: C. Huerta).

The three caves are about 20 metres away from one another and the three of them have independent entrances. You have to anticipate that, if you want to explore the three caves in one dive, you will be going from 12 to 0 metres of depth, with the resulting inconveniences of earache and buoyancy control problems that this may cause, since you will be ascending and descending three consecutive times.

Visibility is usually poor around the whole area, and the caves can be quite dirty. However, the extravagant shapes and colours at the entrance make this dive an enjoyable one.

This is undoubtedly. one of the best dives you can do within the bay of Palma. If you do not have a boat however, you can start the dive from the beach at Marivent; still, I must repeat that it is preferable to enter the caves with someone who knows the caverns' small yet complicated labyrinths. They are not caves to get lost inside, but if you do not have enough experience in cave diving, they can turn out to be somewhat complicated. You must always take at least two torches, and be specially careful with the opening where the breathable vaults are; mind your head! One of the caves reaches so far into the land that the vault is underneath the road that leads to the west dock.

As is frequently the case in caves, there is not much life in these three, but nevertheless there are some brown meagres, goldcrests, prawns, hermit crabs and other characteristic creatures of the dark. Up until a few years ago, at the entrance of the largest cave, the one which is nearest to the beach, there lived a huge grouper; unfortunately in the end it could not withstand the pollution and the harpoons.

POLLENÇA. COVA D'EN JERONI

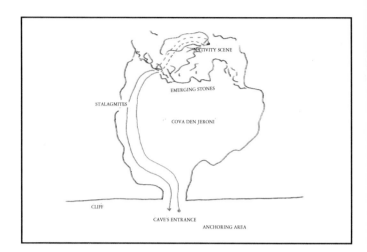

Technique:	medium
Average depth:	9 metres
Maximum depth:	19 metres
Duration:	30 minutes
Difficulties:	locating the cave and anchoring
Recommended season:	summer

The Cova d'en Jeroni is one of the most extraordinary places in Majorca. It is a cavern of spectacularly large proportions to which one can access only by diving from the steep coast of Formentor's cape. The entrance to the cave is not much further after Cala Murta and Cala Gossalba, it is just beyond the Punta del Vent. After having passed this rocky formation you can find a place to anchor under the cliff, about 30 metres away from the vertex of the point. There is nothing on the wall that indicates the entrance to the cave, but a small crack timidly insinuates the place to swim towards in order to notice the "doorway" under the water. Undoubtedly, the Cova d'en Jeroni is still unspoiled precisely because it cannot be seen clearly from the surface or from one of the many boats and yachts that cruise by very close to it.

The nearest port is Port de Pollença, and one of the diving centres that organises diving trips to the Cova d'en Jeroni more often is the Club Tritón in Palma. This club has arranged a small nativity scene inside the cave and it is a tradition among its members to go there around Christmas time and add a new figure each year.

1. Diving in Formentor (Photo: C. Huerta). 2. Spiny lobster (*Palinurus elephas*). Once an abundant crustacean, it is now harder and harder to see (Photo: J. Serra)

Remember that to be able to anchor and dive safely around the cave you must be especially cautious with the sea conditions and aware of the possible changes. Sometimes it has been much easier to get in the cave than to get out of it. It is also convenient not to stay for very long inside the cave because in this area of Majorca the wind and the sea can change quite suddenly.

Entering the cave is relatively easy, you only have to dive (it is done perfectly in apnoea) about ten metres, through a very large "doorway" at about two metres of depth, near the crack that indicates the entrance and which is just after the Punta des Vent. Following the entrance you swim in the crystal clear and tranquil water of the surface of a lake which is about one hundred metres long and one hundred metres wide. As you float inside the Cova, the ceiling of the cave is approximately 30 metres high. The light from the exterior gives the lake a luminescent blue colour, giving you a curious sensation, nearly magic, to see how indescribably illuminated is the water inside the Cova d'en Jeroni. Floating in the lake you can see that, curiously, you do not need a light to see the rocks on the bottom of the cavern, but you do need it to see inside the cave.

When you get to the centre of the lake you can swim to the end of the cave where there is a place suitable to come out of the water and sit on the rocks while you illuminate the cavern with your torches and flashlights. On this sort of rocky islet inside the great vault you can walk a few minutes (be careful as it is very slippery) until the end, where you will see the formations that are characteristic of land caves and the nativity scene made by the members of the Club Tritón.

As well as the visit to the cave it is worthwhile to explore the rocks and stones around the entrance of the cave and which make up most part of the dive.

Experts link up this cave, on the outside, with the Cova de la Columna which is at the other end of the Point; but this is altogether another story.

Yellow parazoa, (*Parazoanthus axinellae*). Abundant hexacorallia in sombre areas. (Photo: C. Huerta)

FORMENTOR. ES COLOMER ISLAND

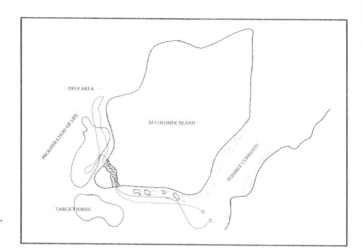

Technique:	medium, high
Average depth:	25 metres
Maximum depth:	40 metres
Duration:	30 minutes
Difficulties:	depth, weather and the lack of shelters
Recommended season:	end of summer and beginning of autumn and only when the weather is very good.

The Colomer island is an impressive 103 metres high crag. It lies west of Cap Formentor, at the far north end of Majorca. The whole of the Colomer island's coast is a very rugged cliff. The diving area is separated from the cape of Formentor by a 70 metres wide channel.

This dive is somewhat difficult because of the depth of the water and the location of the islet.

Taking a small boat, you leave from Port de Pollença. You have to go around and beyond the cape of Formentor, then you arrive to Es Colomer after an interesting and exciting crossing.

The best area for anchoring is at the south of the islet, over a rock substratum, where depth is about 17 metres. This is the ideal place to anchor although not necessarily to dive. So once in the water you swim towards the southwest end of Es Colomer, where a great hole traverses the islet from one side to the other. The underwater landscape is magnificent, as it is all around the northwest coast of Majorca.

You swim through the enticing tunnel that will take you to an area which is very rocky and teeming with the characteristic species of these waters. Sea whips, wreathy-tufts, Sparidae and other species regular in areas with rocks, frequent currents and little contamination, seem to be more alive here than ever.

As you continue moving towards the north, you will arrive to an area where depth is about 40 metres, the coral like shapes predominate and the light is surprisingly intense for this depth.

Do not get too overconfident: it is convenient to keep an eye on the depthfinder and the manometer constantly.

At this depth you can observe small branches of red coral, red sea whips and swallowtail sea perches, red breams, large scaled scorpion fish and, at the bottom of the cracks, greater forkbeards and lobsters. Avoid staying for too long at this depth in order not to accumulate too much nitrogen and start the return route back to the boat reducing your depth gradually and taking pleasure from finding some open sea fish that may appear at any time of the year around the Formentor waters.

The most suitable area for decompression is near the cliff's wall at the Colomer islet, where you will see such molluscs as hervias and peltodoris and all sorts of starfish and anemones.

When you start to return, you will be overwhelmed by the steep coast and the depths of this unspoiled Majorcan area which is still in its natural state.

Above: Sardinie coral (*Corallium rubrum*). As a consequence of the intense harvesting that it is object of, sardinie coral has become rare in our coasts, and it is only present in cracks and caves or at great depths (Photo: J. Serra). Next page: the transparency of the water in some parts of the Balearics, like the Formentor peninsula, is comparable only to some tropical seas (Photo: C. Huerta)

CALA AGULLA. SA MULA

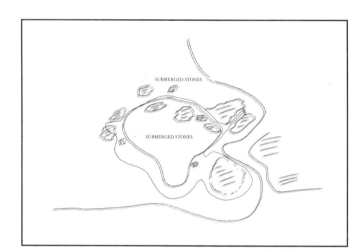

Technique:	medium, high
Average depth:	17 metres
Maximum depth:	24 metres
Duration:	50 minutes
Difficulties:	those of the open sea
Recommended season:	May and June

At sea we call "bank" to a rocky undersea extension that ascends vertically to a plain, without reaching the surface of the water. Because of their capacity to retain particles and other organic matter in suspension, banks are likely to accumulate a great quantity of varied marine life. You could say that they are islands in the bottom of the sea.

One of these banks is the one known as Sa Mula de Cala Agulla, very close to Cala Ratjada, at the north of Majorca. But unfortunately Sa Mula has lost most of the marine life that characterised it because it has little depth and because it is very near the coast, which has made access to it very easy for underwater fishermen.

Groupers used to be very large and numerous in Sa Mula, but today the few that have been able to survive know only too well what mankind means.

The bank is located in the centre of the bay of Cala Agulla, and its coordinates are 39-43,6 N and 003-23,3 E.

You can get to the shallows by boat from Cala Ratjada, where there is a public slipway, or from Cala Lliteres, where the Mero diving club is. At this centre, which is dedicated to non-professio-

1. Launching a boat at the Club Mero in Cala Lliteres (Photo: A. Alonso). 2. Group of seasuckers (*Aplysia depilans*). A large opisthobranchia mollusc that reaches 30 cm in length and one kilo of weight (Photo: C. Huerta).

1. Young Atlantic horse mackerels (*Trachurus trachurus*) between the tentacles of a crimpy jellyfish. 2. Sea bottom in Sa Mula. 3. Crimpy jellyfish (*Cotylorhiza tuberculata*). The tentacles of this jellyfish are frequently used as a refuge to small fish that are not affected by their poison. (Photos: C. Huerta).

nal diving only, they organise outings around all the area and, of course, to the bank of Sa Mula.

Locating the bank will be easy with the help of an echo sounder, alternatively, it is not difficult either if you know how to use the information on a GPS correctly. Sight is also important since the bank can be seen from the surface of the water.

After checking that the anchor is holding well, start the journey by circling around the rocks at the bottom of Sa Mula. The stones descend towards the south, among phanerogams.

Rock fish of surprisingly large sizes are abundant here, specially peacock and rainbow wrasses. Among the males, the *Symphodus tinca* (peacock wrasse) species stands out with its exquisite colours, which are even more brilliant during May and June, their spawning period.

At the more external point of the bank the topography gets more abrupt, originating an accentuated cliff.

At the foot of the slope you are sure to see some members of the scorpion fish family, both large scaled and small red; they stay motionless, lying in wait for prey, protected by their cryptic coloration.

At the safety stop, particularly during the spring and summer months, you will see some species of jellyfish passing close by. These are animals' that multiply with alternating generations of polyps by gemation and jellyfish by sexual reproduction. Some of these species such as *Chrysaora hyoscella* and *Cotylorhiza tuberculata* are very beautiful, although other similar species, such as *Physalia physalis*, can be very dangerous or even cause death. However, not all the jellyfish species cause skin eruptions.

164

CALA SA NAU. SA COVA

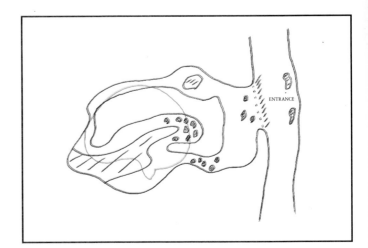

Technique:	medium, high
Average depth:	7 metres
Maximum depth:	10 metres
Duration:	40 minutes
Difficulties:	those of caves
Recommended season:	having little depth, being a short journey and having a protected situation makes it suitable for winter.

Exploring the cave of Cala Sa Nau is not particularly dangerous; its maximum depth is only 10 metres, there are no bifurcations and you can see the light of the cave's exit at all times, nevertheless you need a certain degree of technique to get to the end of the cave comfortably.

Sa Cova is especially interesting because of its stalactitic and stalagmitic formations, belonging to periods when the sea level was lower than it is now and when water dripping continually over the limestone caves moulded spectacular shapes around the coast line.

You have to use a boat to be able to access the diving area. To get to Cala Sa Nau by road, after driving out of the small town of S'Horta and with a small dinghy behind or on top of the car, drive towards Cala Ferrera. After one kilometre you will see a small asphalted track to the left of the road, which will take you to Cala Sa Nau. Launch the boat at the beach. If you have a larger boat however, you can get to the cove from the nearby Porto Colom.

On the left side of the cove, going there by sea, there is a whitish coloured cliff at the beginning of the cove's entrance. After about 150 metres, the cliff loses verticality and height, and just

1. The large scaled scorpion fish (*Scorpaena scrofa*) is a bentonic fish that hunts lying in wait, taking advantage of its colours, which camouflage it with the substrata. 2. Basic cave diving equipment (Photos: C. Huerta).

1. Entrance of the cave. 2. Wreathy-tuft (*Spirographis spallanzanii*) (Photos: C. Huerta). 3. *Cerianthus membranaceus*. 4. The brown meagre (*Sciaena umbra*) is one of the fish most affected by underwater fishing, rarer every year because of its poor ability to react (Photos: A. Alonso).

before a small inlet you will see, on the rock, a large horizontal crack. Right underneath this point and at seven metres of depth is the entrance to the cave of Cala Sa Nau.

Let the anchor down right there, near the entrance of the cave, under the cliff's horizontal crack.

Start the dive by going directly to the cave's entrance. The bottom is sandy and rocky, and the maximum depth is only ten metres.

Enter the cave by the left hand side of the opening and observe the deep cracks that are full of stalactites and stalagmites at the base of the rock wall; it is not hard to find groupers and brown meagres wandering about among these formations.

Explore around the inside of the cave, crossing its main gallery, which is approximately 20 metres long, and then you will find a prominent rock that goes up to 3 metres. This is where you will see, looking backwards, the magnificent display at the entrance, where stalactites and stalagmites stand out against the light. At the centre of the cavity there is an outstanding column. In this part of the cave the ceiling is high and forms a breathable air vault of a relatively large size.

At the end of the cave there is a turning to the right, to an area with a sandy bottom that is inhabited by shrimps, wreathy-tufts and *Cerianthus*.

Before turning around to go back to the entrance, you will see, in one of the bends, additional calcareous formations of great beauty, that stand out in shades and contours, like phantom figures surprised by the flashlights.

THE BAY OF PALMA. ARTIFICIAL REEFS

Technique:	high
Average depth:	28 metres
Maximum depth:	32 metres
Duration:	30 minutes
Difficulties:	the depth
Recommended season:	winter and spring

In the early nineties, the authorities installed groups of artificial reefs in a few places around the bay of Palma, with the object of revitalising the marine fauna, settling the bottom of the bay, and creating manmade areas suitable for the development of marine life. These reefs are made up of various groups of large brick blocks and they are located in the area that lies between Cap Enderrocat and Cap Regana, opposite the Delta Hotel. Their coordinates are: 1 39-27,03 N and L 002-43,01 E.

The reefs are at a depth of 30 metres and the distance to the coast is approximately one mile.

To find the reef's exact point you must use a GPS, alignments or an echo sounder.

The blocks that form the reef are easily recognisable on the echo sounder, because they were sunk over a bottom of algae and sand.

The structures are between two and four metres high, and they are isolated from other rocks or banks that might confuse you.

When you are over this small artificial reef, you can start the dive, not without previously checking the current.

You descend along the anchor chain, taking into account that the sea water here can be somewhat cloudy because of the quality of the sea floor. The dive is therefore vertical, going down to 30 metres.

1. The artificial reefs are built with bricks that form holes of all sizes and which serve as a refuge to many marine species (Photo: A. Alonso). 2. A white bream (*Diplodus sargus*) hides at the bottom of one of the constructions (Photo: C. Huerta).

Depending on the visibility of the day, you might have some difficulties locating the artificial blocks at the bottom.

Once you find them it is important to approach the reefs gently. The brick blocks will appear before you as large quadrangular cubes saturated with holes.

It is better to approach them from above, in order not to disturb the sand at the bottom.

Among the artificial reefs' inhabitants are groupers, brown meagres and white breams, they are very shy and easily frightened, not used to get any visits. That is why you must very carefully come closer to the reef and look around among the hundreds of holes to discover some of the groupers hidden amid the bricks.

This is a peculiar dive, difficult only because of the depth and because locating the reef is a bit complicated. It is remarkable to dive in the sand and posidonia plateau, next to the huge artificial blocks made up of hundreds or even thousands of bricks.

1. Barnacle (*Lepas anatifera*) on the buoy line that up until a few years ago marked the reefs (Photo: C. Huerta). 2. Pilotfish (*Naucrates ductor*) under the buoy that marked the reefs (Photo: C. Huerta)

CALA RATJADA. CAP DES FREU

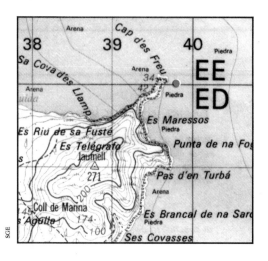

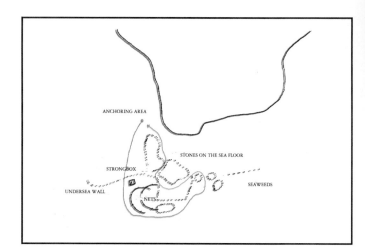

Technique:	high
Average depth:	19 metres
Maximum depth:	30 metres
Duration:	40 minutes
Difficulties:	anchoring and maritime traffic
Recommended season:	May and June

The Cap des Freu dive takes place amid beautiful submerged rocks and stones and a spectacular marine landscape. This cape is at the north of Majorca and its nearest port is Cala Ratjada, where you are most likely to set out from if you have a boat.

At Cala Ratjada there is a public slipway from where a light boat can be launched. From this port to the Cap des Freu there are approximately four marine miles in a direct course, however, if you decide to go along the impeccably clean beaches of Cala Agulla and Cala Moltó there will be one more mile.

When you get to the area of Cap des Freu you must look for the anchoring place at one side or the other of the cape's point, depending on the sea conditions. If you can choose because the conditions are good, try to throw the anchor on the south side of the cape, very close to the coast, and indicating well your condition of divers with Alfa flags or buoys. This is a passageway that many boats, specially during the summer, make use of to short cut their way to the coast. Of course it is imperative to come up to the surface by the anchor chain, and if it were necessary to rise to the surface during the dive, here more than anywhere else, you must do it with a decompression balloon.

The nearest diving centre is Mero, in Cala Lliteres, very near Cala Ratjada. This centre orga-

The turquoise blue waters in Cala Moltó, not far from Cap des Freu (Photo: C. Huerta)

nises dives around the area and they call the Es Freu dive "the strongbox". The name was given to the area of Es Freu because there is a fairly small strongbox resting on the sandy bottom, to which every diver who ignores its existence goes to as soon as he or she sees it. The box is empty and it could be lifted out of the water very easily, but it is already a part of the dive, and amusing to see.

After you anchor, start the itinerary moving lengthwise along the main axis of the cape, reaching the maximum depth at the beginning, which is of 30 metres in the sandy area where the strongbox is. Near the box there are the remains of nets and lines with buoys that could look like fragile submerged vaults. Ascend gently between the rock wall at the bottom, entering the area of stones and cracks that might hide one or two groupers, depending on the day and the time of year; half way down to the bottom you will see amber Jacks, and even some evasive dentexes. Little by little, and observing the required decompression stops, you get to the depth of 14 metres, which in this dive is where there is more life and colour.

The ideal place is just opposite the cape and between 12 and 30 metres of depth. Beyond the cape there is seaweed and sand, and at more than 30 metres of depth there is only sand, although occasionally, some considerably sized sting rays have been seen here.

If the weather is good, the journey to the diving area pleasant, and the sea bottom crystal clear, you will enjoy one of the most colourful and varied dives in the area of Cala Ratjada. It is also advisable to pay attention to the weakly lit holes where with a bit of luck you will see one or two Majorcan lobsters.

1. Spiny lobster (*Palinurus elephas*). 2. Sea cucumber (Photos: C. Huerta)

PORTO CRISTO. SA COVA DES DIMONI

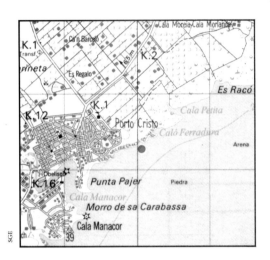

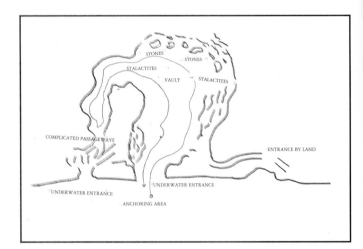

Technique:	high
Average depth:	6 metres
Maximum depth:	15 metres
Duration:	undetermined
Difficulties:	those of caves
Recommended season:	spring

Only a few hundred metres north of Porto Cristo there is the so-called Cova del Dimoni (the devil's cave).

The entrance of this cave is hard to find, but it is well worthwhile to look for it patiently, because Sa Cova is known as one of the best dives you can do in Majorca and it must not be missing in this book of dives around the island.

It is not a specially complicated dive, but it could be somewhat dangerous because of the narrow galleries and areas where you can get trapped. The cave is not large enough to get lost inside; but it is nevertheless wiser to attempt it only if you have enough experience in cave diving.

The origin of such curious name for a cave is unknown, however, some people still maintain today that sporadic satanic masses are celebrated in its enormous breathable vault, which is the size of a basketball court. Tradition has it that these black masses are held by local people and that they get in the cave by land, through a tiny and secret entrance situated in the area where the cliff is. The truth is that it is frequent to find the remains of spent red candles on top of the stalag-

1. Lake inside the Cova del Dimoni (Photo: J. Poyatos). 2. The inside of the cave is spectacular (Photo: A. Alonso)

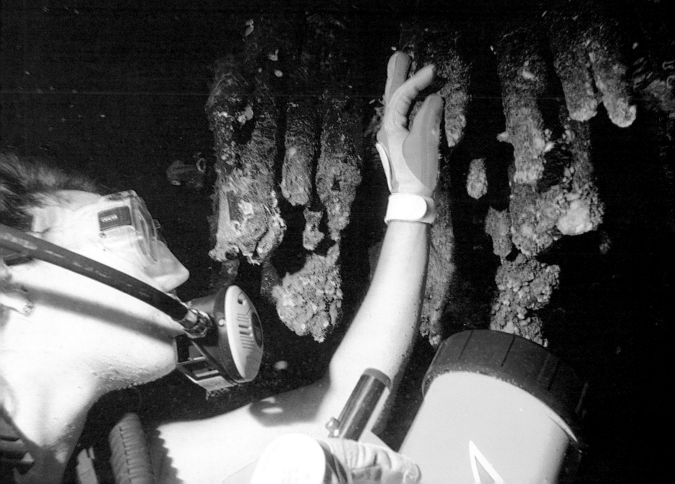

The hermit crab (*Dardanus arrosor*) does not have its own shell, instead it takes on the empty ones it finds. As it grows, it abandons the shell it is living in and finds a larger one that suits it (Photo: C. Huerta).

mites. On the other hand, some divers maintain that occasionally, when they come up to the surface inside the cavern, they have seen people running in the dark, heading towards the hidden galleries.

As we have said before, finding the entrance to the cave is difficult and there are no clear references to be able to describe its position. It is therefore much better to ask one of the staff members at the Albatros diving centre in Cala Millor to brief you on the aspects to take into account to do this special dive. The Triton club of Palma also visits this cavern from time to time.

Someone from Cala Millor's Albatros diving centre will be able to accompany you to the entrance of the cave and serve as a guide around its interior.

Apart from the almost secret entrance used by the mysterious visitors of the cave for their "black masses", the entrance by sea is at more or less 6 metres of depth, along the cliff's wall.

This entrance is large and involves no great difficulty for divers, but as you move forward it gets narrower and bifurcates, making it necessary to be familiarised with it in order to find the right passageway to the area inside where the breathable vault is. The last section has a maximum height of about eight metres from the water surface to the rock ceiling; you could park two buses inside the area with breathable air. It is quite spectacular to see the stalagmites at the bottom of the vault's undersea lake nearly touching the stalactites of the ceiling. Inside this vault you can walk out up to the rocks that serve as a subterranean shore.

Sa Cova is like a stone "theatre", moulded by the filtered water from the surface during millions of years.

Cons

Inside of the cave (Photo: C. Huerta)

SÓLLER. SA COVA DES CAVALL

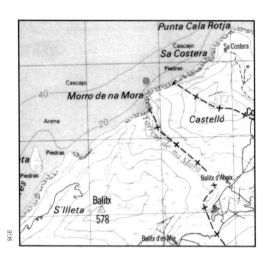

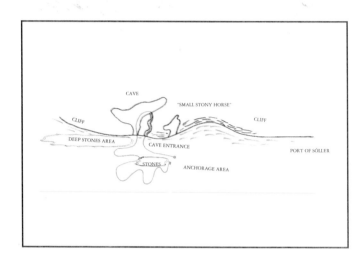

Technique:	medium, (or high if you enter the "chimney")
Average depth:	20 metres
Maximum depth:	24 metres
Duration:	45 minutes
Difficulties:	those of caves
Recommended season:	summer

The so-called Cova des Cavall (horse's cave) lies northeast from the port of Sóller. The Cova des Cavall is specially attractive because it is a cavern with independent entrance and exit openings. The horse's cave has a chimney on one end that takes you to a very narrow air chamber where you can breathe.

The whole cavern is gentle for easy going and careful divers, except for the chimney, which can turn into a nasty trap. Only one diver at a time can barely go through this very narrow and vertical gallery. It is impossible to turn around inside the chimney and you have to get to the end of it to be able to turn around. The cave and the

gallery at the end are quite short. You must remember that only a maximum of three divers can go into the gallery at one time.

The horse's cave is north of the port of Sóller and the nearest diving centre is Octopus, its address is Canonge Oliver street, at the port. Octopus organises group outings, rents equipment and refills air cylinders.

Departing from the port of Sóller by boat, cover about four miles bordering the coast towards the northeast. Go beyond Ses Puntes and S'Illeta and, before arriving to the mouth of the Torrent de na Mora, you will see a large stone in the shape of a horse's head on the rocky wall of the coast: this is the anchoring spot.

About thirty metres away from the horse's head, towards the coast, you notice the entrance to the cave from the surface of the water.

Anchoring is relatively easy and the depth is about 20 metres. Beware of the possible swing at anchor and the rocky wall.

Descend along the anchor chain and head towards the coast's wall, where the cave is. The maximum depth at this point is of about 26 metres. At the base of the wall and the entrance to the cave the depth is approximately 20 metres. The entrance is wide and allows divers to swim next to one another during the first few metres. Flashlights or torches are obviously necessary, however, in case of an emergency you can come out of the cave with the natural light of the two entrance openings. The cave continues getting narrower and bending upwards a few times. At the deepest part of the cave is the chimney's small entrance. You must be extremely careful during this part, it can only be done if you control the feeling of claustrophobia. The chimney is very narrow and it ascends among pointy rocks towards a breathable opening. At the end of this chimney there is a vault, where a maximum of two or three divers can be at the same time. Turning around is complicated, but you can go back safely taking great care while you advance along the four metres long chimney. The dive to the horse's cave is easy if you do not intend to go into the chimney. The marine life is extremely abundant outside the cave, and the large rocks of the sea floor turn this diving experience into a memorable venture.

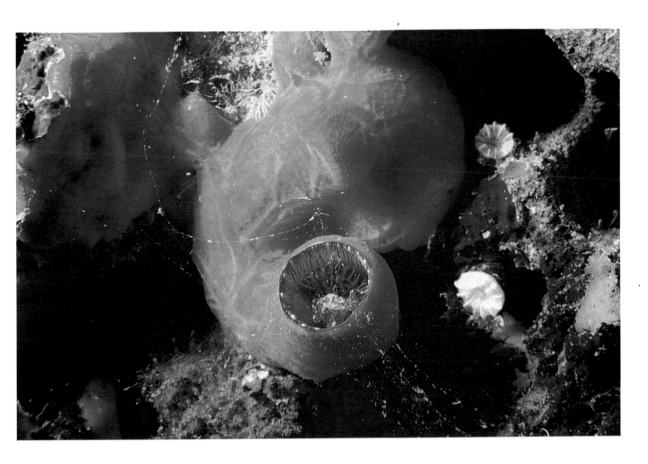

Crambe crambe (Photo: C. Huerta)

1. Exploring an undersea gallery (Photo: C. Huerta). 2. Crab (*Dromia vulgaris*) (Photo: A. Alonso). 3. If you stay very still, the fish will come closer to investigate (Photo: C. Huerta)

CABRERA. PUNTA DEL DIMONI

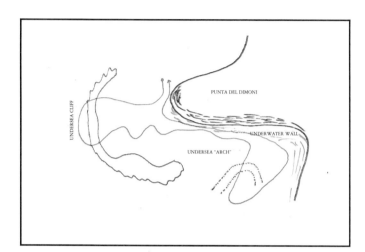

Technique:	medium
Average depth:	18 metres
Maximum depth:	32 metres
Duration:	45 minutes
Difficulties:	area with currents
Recommended season:	summer and autumn

This is without doubt one of the three or four best dives you can do around the Balearic Islands. It is an explosion of light and life. The sea floor is extraordinary and the rock shapes amazing.

At the north of the island of Cabrera there is the Punta del Dimoni, opposite the Redona island, near Cala Ganduf.

You anchor facing the point and start the dive towards the sea, as if you were going to the Redona island. You will immediately see an underwater cliff which you can follow and explore, marvelling at the abundance of enormous white breams, groupers (the whole of Cabrera is full of them) and many considerably sized barracudas.

When you have recovered from the surprise of the undersea cliff's breathtaking sight, go back towards the Punta del Dimoni. Go around the point along its west side and contemplate the amazing sculptured shapes on the abundant stones full of corals of all sorts. There are thousands of living filtering organisms here, such as sponges, sea whips and wreathy-tufts that, gripping onto the point's rocks, live oblivious to contamination.

The area is always teeming with life thanks to the channel's currents, and during this dive you may be surprised by large pelagic specimens, such as short sunfish or even tunas.

Divers checking the equipment one last time before they dive in the blue waters of the National Park of Cabrera (Photo: A. Alonso)

Towards Cabrera at sunset, the first islets can be seen in the horizon (Photo: A. Alonso).

After bordering the point you will see, as the culmination of visual pleasure, the great undersea "monument" in the shape of an arch of triumph that invites you to go through its gigantic columns. At this point you must pay special attention to the dentexes, who like to observe the divers' nervous and clumsy movements.

No one, no matter how much diving experience he or she might have in tropical seas, will remain indifferent towards so much beauty and exuberant life. This is probably what the Mediterranean looked like before the arrival of human beings. The only human vestiges left in this part of Cabrera are the remains of nets, entrapped forever like drapery, in the undersea arch. There are also many pieces of amphorae and sunken ceramics in the cove, the unequivocal sign of the passage of unlucky sailors who lost the battle against the sea.

Before you realise it, it will be time to return, and you have to go back the same way, decreasing your depth and observing at length the anemones and the corals at the edge of the Punta del Dimoni's cliff.

No photographic camera can reflect the arch of triumph's light and colours like they deserve. The flashlight will not be necessary during this dive, because Cabrera's luminosity and visibility here are at their very best.

It is advisable to do this dive within one of the outings organised by the Isurus diving centre, in Palma. They are the most experienced in the incomparable sea bottom of Cabrera.

This dive is absolutely essential for any diver.

1. Crab (*Maja Verrucosa*). Its body is usually covered with seaweeds and polyp colonies. (Photo: C. Huerta). 2. The Castle of Cabrera, at the entrance of the main port of the island (Photo: A. Alonso).

CABRERA. CAP LLEBEIG... GROUPERS AND GROUPERS

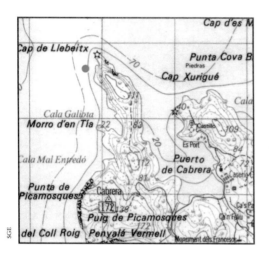

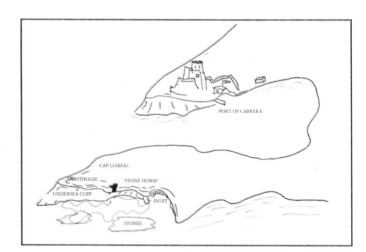

Technique:	medium
Average depth:	20 metres
Maximum depth:	35 metres
Duration:	60 minutes
Difficulties:	anchoring and weather changes
Recommended season:	in summer there are more groupers, in spring and autumn you might see large pelagic species

The archipelago of Cabrera alone deserves an entire book written about it. Its singular history, its fauna and its specific legislation for non-professional diving practices make these islands a very special area indeed. Cabrera lies south of Cap Salines, about three miles southeast of Majorca. To go diving around Cabrera – at the moment the only Spanish maritime and land national park – it is necessary to make a specific request at the park's offices in Palma, the headquarters of which are in Plaza de España. Apart from the diving permission request, you have to fill in an application form for the boat, where you need to give the

details of both the boat and the skipper. When you arrive to Cabrera you are required to moor at the port and hand in the authorisations at the park's offices. After that you can go to the authorised diving areas.

Head towards Cala Galiota at the northeast of the island, and anchor before you get there, after you have turned Cap Llebeig, more or less 20 metres away from the cliff, which is 110 metres high. The depth here is around 30 metres. Bear in mind that at only 200 metres from the Cap Llebeig you can find depths of up to 100 metres.

Now that the boat is anchored at approxima-

190

Cons

Playing with a small grouper (*Epinephelus guaza*) (Photo: A. Alonso)

tely 450 metres north from the Morro d'en Tià, 20 metres away from the shore, and under a rock on the cliff that looks like a sea horse, you can start the dive according to the current. Go to the maximum depth, about 35 metres, at the beginning of the dive. At this depth there are large rocks where spectacularly large groupers live. You are diving just below where the sea horse shaped rock on the cliff is. Decreasing the depth gradually, head towards Cap Llebeig. After covering a convenient distance, always according to the sea conditions and to the amount of air you have left in the cylinders, start the return closer to the shore, under the cliff. Finish the itinerary at not much depth, coming up near the sea horse. Do not fail to observe the huge barracudas that live in these waters and who will feel attracted by your presence.

During the summer, the groupers are even more abundant and they are easily three times larger, some of them weighing up to 30 kilos. The largest groupers will hardly ever approach you, but the smaller ones do come out to greet the divers. The reproduction cycle of the groupers is unique because they are all born female, and only after they reach a certain maturity – approximately when they weigh 3 kilos – they change their sex turning into males, and then they live apart. It is also known that groupers normally weigh one kilo more each year.

To do any dive around Cabrera it is convenient to consult first at the Tritón club or at the Centro Subacuático Isurus of Palma. Also, at these centres they organise dives in Cabrera all year round.

At Tritón or at Isurus they will inform you thoroughly about the places where visiting is allowed in Cabrera and the necessary procedures to get the required authorisations.

It is not unusual to see dolphins and other habituals of the open sea in the channel of Cabrera (Photo: A. Alonso).

1. Preparing the dive in Cap Llebeig. 2. Few places have the abundance of groupers that Cabrera has (Photos: A. Alonso).

THE BAY OF PALMA. THE ALMAGRO SUNKEN WRECK

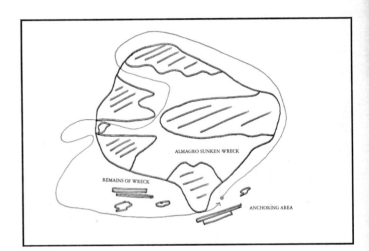

ALMAGRO SUNKEN WRECK

REMAINS OF WRECK

ANCHORING AREA

Technique:	high
Average depth:	34 metres
Maximum depth:	36 metres
Duration:	15 minutes at the bottom, plus the decompression
Difficulties:	anchoring, weather changes and large congers
Recommended season:	beginning of autumn, because in summer the marine breeze reaches enough strength to raise the sea, and in winter a very cold current makes the dive inadvisable.

Facing the cove of Portals Vells there is a Phoenician vessel resting on the bottom of the sea since the IV century BC. The boat is practically fossilised on the sand bed and its shape is not clearly that of a boat, instead it looks like an enormous rock in the shape of a 10 metres long vessel. The dive cannot be considered easy, because the sunken wreck is at 36 metres of depth, there are currents, and both the descent and the ascent necessarily imply making decompression stops; but the noteworthy scene of such ancient remains of objects is worth the while. Studies of this boat,

that sank just before arriving to Majorca, were completed in the early 70s. Its exact origin and the cause for its sinking are unknown, although some people speculate that it must have caught fire.

The wreck is not easy to find and it is better to make this dive with someone who knows the area well. The exact coordinates are: l 30-28,28 N and L 002-31,97 E.

The nearest diving centre is Calumet, below the Bonanza Hotel in Illetas. You can do this dive with the Calumet centre or from your own boat.

The nearest place to launch a pneumatic dinghy into the water is the beach at Portals Vells, but it is convenient to bear in mind that in summer the beach is packed with tourists from 10 o'clock in the morning.

The dive has to start with a direct descent in a somewhat cloudy water, specially in summer. Also bear in mind that the thermal wind at the end of the morning can change the appearance and safety of the sea in the bay of Palma.

The Phoenician wreck, known as the Almagro wreck, has the added attraction of the enormous congers that live inside the ancient boat.

Today, the remains of the boat are an enormous rock where a large conger of about two metres known as "Sebastian" lives and usually comes out to greet the divers looking for a bit of food. Sebastian is not dangerous, but it is nevertheless better not to make it nervous by getting too close or trying to touch it. Near Sebastian's cave there are other considerably large congers, it has even been said that there is one particularly huge and unpleasant conger, assuring it is 3 metres long and that it only comes out at night.

You can find the position of the sunken wreck by aligning the Sec island with the Valparaiso hotel in Palma, and the west point of Portals Vells cove with a sort of column at the far side of the cove. A third alignment can be taken aligning the west extremity of the Casino building with the beginning of a luxury residence over the Punta de S'Estaca.

Apart from these alignments and the GPS, it is convenient to use an echo sounder to anchor close to the wreck.

Remember that this is not an easy dive by any standards, and that a surprise encounter with Sebastian and its friends at 36 metres of depth could be the beginning of a nasty experience.

The remains of a sunken amphora together with other relics of an ancient shipwreck (Photo: A. Alonso).

CALA AGULLA. THE CATHEDRAL CAVE

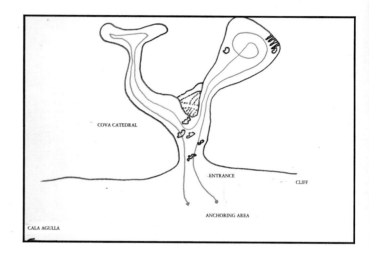

Technique:	high
Average depth:	9 metres
Maximum depth:	19 metres
Duration:	30 minutes
Difficulties:	those of caves
Recommended season:	May and June

The "Cathedral" cave is possibly one of the most magnificent dives one can do in the Balearic islands, but it is also one of the most difficult, therefore you must remember that in order to attempt this dive it is preceptive to have the necessary qualifications that entitle you to practice cave diving.

It is called the Cathedral cave because it is one of the most dramatic undersea caves in Majorca, in view of its size and its numerous formations that are full of huge columns stalagmites and stalactites. Diving in between its galleries and tunnels is like flying over them.

To get to the Cathedral you have to use a boat

that you can launch from the public slipway at Cala Ratjada, the nearest port. Heading towards the northwest as you come out of that port, you have to advance about three miles parallel to the coast until you have passed the lovely beaches of Cala Agulla and Cala Moltó. After you have gone past the point of Na Foguera start looking for a small inlet with a fissure on the rock that timidly indicates the entrance to the Cathedral cave.

Anchor very carefully because the weather or the sea conditions could change suddenly. The boat has to stay near the crack on the cliff that serves as an indicator of the entrance to the cave.

It is really important to be accompanied by an

1. Entrance to the cave (Photo: C. Huerta). 2. Prawn (*Palaemon elegans*) (Photo: C. Huerta).

Large chamber with breathable air at the end of the main gallery. This is undoubtedly one of the largest and most impressive underwater caves of the island. In order to explore it you must have a suitable license and go with a guide or a specialised cave diving instructor (Photo: C. Huerta).

experienced diver who knows the Cathedral well. One of the centres that visits the Cathedral more often is the Mero club from Cala Ratjada, which is not far from the cave and has been organising dives to the Cathedral for years.

The entrance is large and at not too deep, although once inside the cave and when you advance through it, the entrance seems to be small. Beyond the entrance and progressing towards the dimly illuminated area, your sight will get used and you will distinguish a few galleries. Before you advance any more, tie up the indispensable Ariadna string at the beginning of the right hand side gallery. It seems narrow but it gets wider as it gets deeper. Only a few minutes after entering the water you will already be at the end of the cave's right hand side gallery.

This gallery, which is probably the most beautiful, ends about 60 metres away from the entrance. What started as a narrow tunnel has slowly turned into an ample cavern with a large breathable chamber at the end. Here you can rest for a while, nearly sixty metres away from the entrance and in a cave that still remains practically intact. After a short chat and a readjustment of your equipment, return to the entrance of the gallery along the same way, following the diver who is gathering the string.

After tying up the string again at the entrance of the second gallery, start to explore this part of the cave. In this gallery there are a number of passages, more galleries and narrow paths, which are attractive but they could prove dangerous if you are not careful.

CAP DES LLAMP. THE TUNNEL SHAPED CAVE

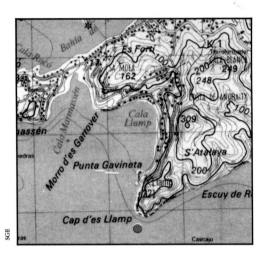

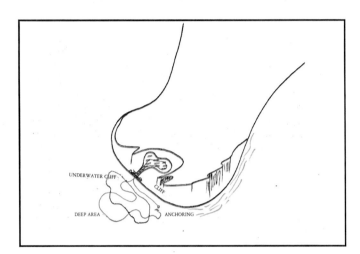

Technique:	high
Average depth:	18 metres
Maximum depth:	33 metres
Duration:	50 minutes
Difficulties:	the muddy bottom of the cave and its narrowness
Recommended season:	spring

Cap des Llamp (cape of lightning) is between Port d'Andratx and Santa Ponça. It is a rugged cape that reaches a height of about 300 metres above the sea level, and just under the point of this great mass is the underwater cave of Cap des Llamp.

This is a relatively easy cave to explore; it starts with a very large entrance that gets narrower as you advance, until it turns into a kind of gallery that comes out to a large cavity where a few divers can enter at the same time.

Anchoring in Cap des Llamp is easy and the place where the cave is situated is clearly defined by a large "V" right at the edge of the cape. You can anchor under this large "V" and start the dive by going directly to the cave in order to have the maximum amount of air reserves when you go inside it.

It is better to go into the cave by pairs. More than two people at one time can cause the slime at the bottom to stir. You must try to enter very slowly, obviously with spare torches and flashlights. It is not necessary to use a safety spool or string, because there is only one exit and it is virtually impossible to get lost.

The cave is spacious at the entrance, but the gallery gets narrower halfway through, to the point that some heavy divers will not be able to go through.

202

To explore the Cova des Llamp is nearly a mystical experience. The special configuration of its entrance as well as the cave's first metres will put your concentration ability and your buoyancy control competence to the test.

No cave has to be done with more calmness and serenity than this one, it is really difficult not to stir the slime at the bottom. Your movements have to be remarkably smooth, and your air consumption is reduced because advancing inside the cave has to be very slow. You must control your buoyancy to stay close to the ceiling of the cave. The most difficult part is an eight metre passageway, the narrowness of which forces you to brush against the walls and ceiling. At this point there are some divers who want to turn around..... but cannot!, because there is not enough space to turn; you have to either get to the end of the tunnel or do not enter the gallery's narrow passage in the first place.

If you have managed to overcome the impression of the passage's narrowness and you have not stirred the bottom excessively, you will find your reward at the end, where there is one last cavity that becomes a large room and from where you can see the inside of the Cap des Llamp. In this room there are 16 metres of rock over your heads to get to the sea level, and 309 metres to the top of the cape. It is a remarkable experience to enter an undersea cave that allows you to get right inside the cape, down to the bottom of its "soul". Penetrating the rock in such a peculiar way also allows you to reach your own soul, and perhaps that is precisely where the secret of the pleasure of diving lies.

Thanks to harmony and self-control you can reach the inside of the massive rock's cave, down to the rocky depths of the great Cap des Llamp. It is hard to find a similar sensation out of the water.

Impressive close-up of an Abalone (*Haliotis tuberculata*) (Photo: C. Huerta).

THE BAY OF PALMA. THE WEST DOCK'S SUNKEN WRECK

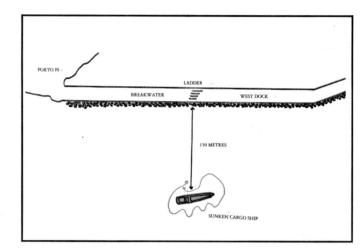

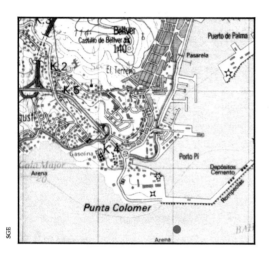

Technique:	high
Average depth:	24 metres
Maximum depth:	27 metres
Duration:	40 minutes
Difficulties:	maritime traffic
Recommended season:	winter

On the outer edge of the west dock, on the south side of the port of Palma, there are a few modern wrecks of considerable size, a real pleasure for divers.

One of these sunken wrecks is at 27 metres of depth and only 150 metres away from the south breakwater of the west dock. It is a modern 60 metres long cargo ship that was sunk intentionally. It lies on the bottom of the water parallel to the breakwater.

You have to get to the diving area by boat. You could access the wreck from the breakwater, but that would be very dangerous because of the intense maritime traffic.

The nearest diving centre is Calumet, below the Bonanza hotel in Illetas. At this centre, apart from imparting courses, refilling the cylinders and hiring equipment, they organise daily outings all around the bay of Palma and most importantly, they know the sunken wrecks of the west dock very well.

Anchor about 150 metres away from the dock's south breakwater and perpendicularly to it, just opposite an old metal ladder.

Descend along the anchor line.

Be careful with the anchor, it could easily drag along the bottom. It is advisable to check on the anchor when you descend.

Propeller of the cargo ship, sunken in the west dock waters, near the entrance to the Port of Palma (Photo: C. Huerta).

Divers on the wreck's deck. You can appreciate the cloudiness of the water, which rarely allow divers to see the dimensions of the whole sunken wrecks (Photo: C. Huerta).

If you have an echo sounder you can find the wreck more easily; if not, you may need to do more than one dive to find it; alternatively, you can hire a guide.

If you know the area well you could at the same time visit this wreck and also a smaller one which is not far from it and which is described in another chapter.

When you get to the old sunken cargo ship, you should normally start by exploring the deck.

The visibility around the wreck is always quite cloudy because the bottom is sandy and slimy. It is important to start by exploring the deck and then advance towards the bottom gradually and very carefully in order not to stir the slime.

You can get inside the bridge and onto the lower deck. The wreckage seems to be well settled and it is not particularly dangerous. There is not much life around, but during spring and summer you will see amber Jacks and wreathy - tufts that look like miniature palm forests, standing in wait for the food that the currents bring.

Remember that even if the depth is not too great, the sunken wreck will absorb and captivate you, and it could easily happen that you will need to make decompression stops on the way up.

Avoid coming out to the surface too far away from the boat, since the maritime traffic of large boats with deep drafts is very intense.

THE BAY OF PALMA. SUNKEN CARGO SHIP AND SAILING YACHT

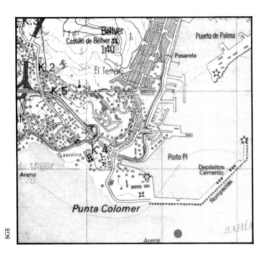

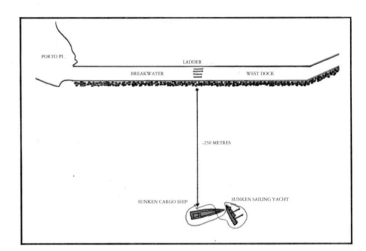

Technique:	high
Average depth:	20 metres
Maximum depth:	28 metres
Duration:	40 minutes
Difficulties:	maritime traffic
Recommended season:	winter

On the outer edge of the west dock, in the port of Palma, there are a few large sunken shipwrecks. One of these wrecks was intentionally sunk during the 80s. It is an approximately 40 metres long multipurpose cargo ship and it has kept in good shape.

To get to the diving area you must go by boat.

The cargo ship is about 250 metres away from the breakwater and it is only possible to find it with an echo sounder and a GPS, or by very carefully aligning the metal ladder on the breakwater, with the golden GESA building in the coast of Palma.

In a reduced area there are four large sunken shipwrecks; although in spite of their size, they are sometimes hard to find because of the poor visibility.

When you arrive to the place where the wreck is, descend along the anchor line. Maximum depth is of about 28 metres and, if you have anchored right above the cargo ship, you will start seeing its silhouette when you get to 18 metres of depth.

The nearest diving centre is Calumet, at the Bonanza hotel in Illetas.

The cargo ship lies in its natural position, its deck is open and you can explore around the inside of the bridge.

It is necessary to take precautions and not to enter the wrecks without a guide or instructor (Photo: C. Huerta).

The ship has right at its bow a sunken sailing yacht of about 14 metres in length that can also be visited safely.

There is not much life around these two shipwrecks, but you can observe some oysters and other creatures that are commonly seen in any sunken wreck.

Visibility is usually poor, so you must pay attention to the rest of the group members, especially during the way back to the boat.

The inside of the cargo ship is absolutely full of lines and cables that will force you to move with extreme precaution. In some parts of the hull there are nets that are hardly visible, blended in with the walls and mistaken for them easily. You have to avoid getting entangled.

Only enter the ship if you are very experienced or if you have a good guide who knows these wrecks. In spite of all the precautions, it is always dangerous to go into any sunken shipwreck.

As a rule of thumb, do not enter the ship in large groups; maybe one after the other, keeping a cautious distance between divers, only going in when the last one has come out, and keeping an eye on your companions at all times.

The way back to the surface has to be done taking into account the possibility of having to stop for decompression. It is very important to emerge next to the anchor line, since the maritime traffic, specially during the summer, is very intense.

This dive requires a certain level of technique. It should be done during a clear day with good visibility.

One of the ship's winches (Photo: A. Alonso).

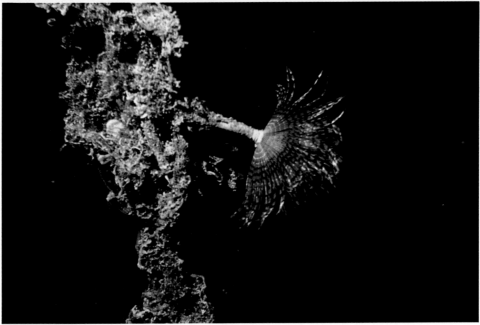

1. Looking through a gap (Photo: C. Huerta). 2. Wreathy-tuft (*Spirographis spallanzanii*) on one of the ship's lines, area where they are strangely abundant. Oysters have started to appear on the sides of the ship in the last few years (Photo: A. Alonso).

DRAGONERA. CAP LLEBEIG

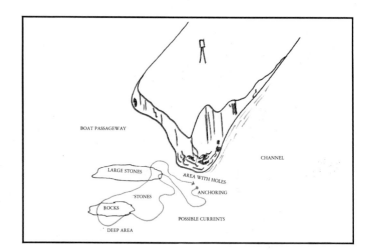

Technique:	high
Average depth:	25 metres
Maximum depth:	38 metres
Duration:	40 minutes
Difficulties:	great depth and strong currents
Recommended season:	spring and beginnings of summer

The island of Dragonera is situated at the west of Majorca, separated from it by a channel which is approximately one mile wide, with strong and frequent currents. This is an area where Carthaginians, Morisco pirates and all sorts of sailors were already foundering many years ago.

Here the sea can change all of a sudden, there are hidden crags only a few centimetres below the water surface, and the coastline is very rugged; but it is also a privileged place for non-professional diving.

The cape of Llebeig is a great mass of rock located at the southwest side of Dragonera. It is an area of rocks where waves break and where the waters are very deep. Whales and sharks have been seen and catalogued not far from the cape.

The nearest port apart from the port at Dragonera is the port of Andratx. At this port there is a petrol station and a public slipway from where small boats can be launched.

From Dragonera, the nearest place to put the boat in at a port is the small jetty of Sant Elm, just a few miles away from Cap Llebeig. The Llebeig dive starts after anchoring just at the south projection of the islet.

The boat will stay anchored close to the cliff,

Moray eel (*Muraena helena*). Despite their fierce appearance, they only bite to defend themselves.
(Photo: J. Serra)

Diver boat at the foot of Cap Llebeig. A certain discipline and organisation, as well as a correct planning, is necessary in any group dive. The Club Tritón does dives around the entire Balearic coast within an annual activity program. (Photo: C. Huerta)

and the descent, after checking the current, will occur between the open sea on the south and the cliff on the north.

It is very important to verify the currents and the anchoring, specially during the summer when the thermal winds cause currents and water fluxes between the channel and the islet.

Descending along the anchor line you will easily reach 20 metres of depth.

Swim towards the northwest, going around the cape, and you will find a cliff that descends from 20 metres down to 40, and it can reach even lower depths in some parts.

The sensation, thanks to the reference points of the undersea cliff, is like free falling. You must pay special attention to the depth; in some parts

of the southwest of Dragonera there are 50 metres of depth at the edge of the cliffs.

The marine fauna at the bottom of Cap Llebeig is the usual fauna of the coast, standing out though are the enormous large scaled scorpion fish and moray eels. In addition, the favourable combination between the strait of Dragonera and the open sea lends itself to the observation in this area of some rare pelagic fish.

The itinerary along the bottom of the underwater cliff and the attractiveness of the place must not make you forget that you will probably need to make a long and slow ascent to liberate nitrogen,

A difficult and impressive dive, only suitable for experienced divers with a good knowledge of diving in deep waters.

1. Tube worm (Photo: C. Huerta). 2. Fish and diver coming together. 3. A grand large scaled scorpion fish (*Scorpaena scrofa*). With its sharp spines it inoculates a poison which can cause strong pains (Photo: J. Serra).

DRAGONERA. THE MOST VORACIUOS CONGER EELS

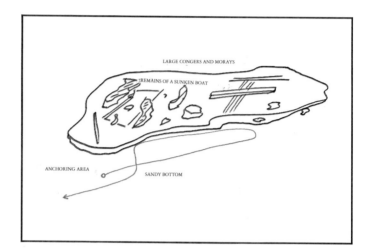

Technique:	very high
Average depth:	34 metres
Maximum depth:	36 metres
Duration:	28 minutes
Difficulties:	location and the conger's aggressiveness
Recommended season:	summer

In the channel between Sant Elm and Dragonera there are the remains of a sunken shipwreck of more or less 20 metres in length. It serves as a refuge for twenty or so congers and eels of an imposing size. The sunken wreck is completely ruined and what is left of it is practically only a heap of scrap with several holes.

Its coordinates are: l 39-34,69 N and L 002-20,07 E.

This is probably the most difficult and dangerous dive one can do around Majorca. The conger and moray eels that live in the wreck are really aggressive, they have got used to the divers and their diet is based essentially on the food that these divers take to their sanctuary.

Occasionally you may find the congers very pacific and relaxed, but sometimes, specially in winter or when they have gone without food for a long time, they seem to demand their food and leap out desperately towards the shocked visitors. Several accidents have already occurred among divers when the congers charge frantically against the hands of those who take them some fish; there have been some attacks and bad bites that have resulted in considerable wounds on the hands and the face. What is really dangerous about these biting episodes is that they can cause panic attacks among the divers, and then these alarmed

BS

Cons

219

divers want to get away fast by going up to the surface, with the risk of suffering accidents such as lung over-expansion or decompression.

It is vital to stay calm at all times and to maintain a certain safety distance between you and the congers in the shipwreck. Some specimens can be very large, as long as two meters, and they live there all year round. The nearby diving centres do regular dives to the wreck all through the summer months. One of the centres that offers more security for this particular dive is the Aquamarine centre. At Aquamarine they use a suitable boat and they anchor safely over the sunken wreck. The instructors install a specially designed floating marker above the anchor, and attach an 18 litre cylinder with six regulators at seven metres of depth onto the anchor line. They also have an auxiliary pneumatic dinghy that they tie a few metres away from the bow of the boat so they can make a fast emergency evacuation if the case arises. This dive has to be done taking all the conceivable safety measures and it must only be attempted if you are a highly proficient diver; it is also essential to respect the conger and moray eels in their habitat. Bold divers will not last long without wounds. The location of the wreck has to be done with alignments or with a GPS, you cannot trust the echo sounder because it will hardly read the depth and the rui-

ned wreck without clear outlines. To fix correctly your position with alignments you line up the right hand side end of the Pantaleu island and a building with arch shaped windows that is further away, in the town. Also line up the cape of Punta Galinda with a long apartment building that is behind it.

1-3. Alignments to locate the wreck with the congers (Photos: A. Alonso). 4-5. The unnatural concentration of congers (*Conger conger*) and morays (*Muraena helena*) and the common practice of feeding, which has many critics, cause a wild whirlpool that makes this dive an exciting and unique experience (Photos: A. Alonso).

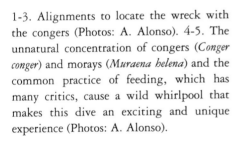

RECOMMENDED CLUBS, SCHOOLS AND DIVING CENTRES

1	Albatros	Cala Santanyí	9	Centro SSI	Baleares
2	Mero	Cala Ratjada	10	Tritón	Palma de Mallorca
3	Albatros Sub	Cala Millor	11	Isurus	Palma de Mallorca
4	Albatros	Cala Figuera	12	U.C.N.	Port Adriano
5	Calumet	Illetes	13	Octopus	Sóller
6	Llevant	Porto Petro	14	Daedalus	Port Adriano
7	Escuba	Santa Ponça	15	Scuba Pollentia	Port de Pollença
8	CPIAS Nico Sport	Porto Cristo			

DIVING CENTRES

NAME OF CENTRE:	Albatros
LOCATION:	Cala Santanyí
MANAGER OR PROPRIETOR:	Francisco Belmonte and Gabriel Ribas
MANAGER'S QUALIFICATIONS:	Instructor
ADDRESS:	Hotel Pinos Playa. Cala Santanyí
OPENING HOURS:	9.00 to 18.00
TELEPHONE:	971 65 39 00
LANGUAGES SPOKEN:	Catalan, Spanish, German, English, French, Italian
BOAT:	7 metres long rigid inflatable boat
OTHER SERVICES:	No
ACCOMMODATION:	Hotel Pinos Playa
CRUISES:	No
QUALIFICATIONS AND COURSES:	Fedas, Padi, Camas
ASSOCIATION:	Club de Actividades Subacuáticas F.E.B.A.S.
DISCOUNTS:	10% for groups of more than 10 people
OTHER INFORMATION:	The centre is at the cove itself

NAME OF CENTRE:	Mero
TOWN:	Cala Ratjada
MANAGER OR PROPRIETOR:	Jaime Ferriol
MANAGER'S QUALIFICATIONS:	CMAS*** and others
ADDRESS:	Cala Lliteres, Cala Agulla
OPENING HOURS:	9.30 to 18.00 hours
TELEPHONE:	971 56 54 67 (from the 1st of May to the 1st of November)
LANGUAGES SPOKEN:	German, English, French, Catalan and Spanish
BOAT:	7,5 metres and 115 HP (longest trip 10 minutes)
OTHER SERVICES:	Scooters Apollo
ACCOMMODATION:	It can be arranged
CRUISES:	No
QUALIFICATIONS AND COURSES:	Night classes, caves, rescue, etc.
ASSOCIATION:	SSI, Barakuda, VDST, Padi, VETL, CMAS, etc.
DISCOUNTS:	Groups of more than 25 people

NAME OF CENTRE:	C.A.S. Albatros Sub
LOCATION:	Cala Millor
MANAGER OR PROPRIETOR:	Antonio Tocornal and Gabriel Ribas
MANAGER'S QUALIFICATIONS:	Instructor
ADDRESS:	C/ Castell s/n Hotel Marina Park
OPENING HOURS:	9.00 to 18.00 hours
TELEPHONE:	971 58 64 22
LANGUAGES SPOKEN:	Spanish, Catalan, German, English, Italian and French
BOAT:	6 metres long rigid inflatable boat, fits 12 people
OTHER SERVICES:	No
ACCOMMODATION:	Hipotel hotels
CRUISES:	No
QUALIFICATIONS AND COURSES:	Fedas, Vets, Cmas
ASSOCIATION:	Club de Actividades Subacuáticas F.E.B.A.S.
DISCOUNTS:	10 % for groups of 10 people
OTHER INFORMATION:	Free transportation to and from the hotel

NAME OF CENTRE:	Albatros
LOCATION:	Cala Figuera. Santanyí
MANAGER OR PROPRIETOR:	Thomas Bewer, Francisco Belmonte and Gabriel Ribas
MANAGER'S QUALIFICATIONS:	Instructor
ADDRESS:	Pier No.7. Fishing port Cala Figuera
OPENING HOURS:	9.00 to 18.00 hours
TELEPHONE:	971 64 53 00
LANGUAGES SPOKEN:	Catalan, Spanish, German and English
BOAT:	6 metres long rigid inflatable boat
OTHER SERVICES:	No
ACCOMMODATION:	Hotel Rocamar
CRUISES:	No
QUALIFICATIONS AND COURSES:	Fedas, Vit, Vets
ASSOCIATION:	Club de Actividades Subacuáticas F.E.B.A.S.
DISCOUNTS:	10 % for groups of 10 people

NAME OF CENTRE:	Calumet Diving S.L.
LOCATION:	Illetes. Calviá
MANAGER OR PROPRIETOR:	Alvaro Garí
MANAGER'S QUALIFICATIONS:	Instructor. MAPA, CMAS
ADDRESS:	Hotel Bonanza. Paseo Illetes s/n - 07015-Calviá
OPENING HOURS:	9.30 to 21.00 hours
TELEPHONE:	971 40 11 12 and 908 333 090 Fax: 971 40 40 50
LANGUAGES SPOKEN:	Catalan, Spanish, English, German
BOAT:	13 seat rigid inflatable boat
OTHER SERVICES:	Equipment refill, retail and hire
ACCOMMODATION:	Hotel Bonanza
CRUISES:	No
QUALIFICATIONS AND COURSES:	P.A.D.I.

NAME OF CENTRE:	Centro Turístico de Buceo Llevant, S.L.
LOCATION:	Porto Petro
MANAGER OR PROPRIETOR:	Antonio Llinás and Miguel Rigo
MANAGER'S QUALIFICATIONS:	Three star instructor
OPENING HOURS:	9.00 to 19.00 hours
TELEPHONE:	971 67 70 12 Fax: 971 64 36 36
LANGUAGES SPOKEN:	German, English, French, Catalan, Spanish
BOAT:	20 metres, 90 seat Golondrina type, and a RIB
OTHER SERVICES:	Cylinder refill, accommodation arrangement
ACCOMMODATION:	Hotels Talayal, Marthas, Dolce Farniente
CRUISES:	Cabrera National Park (organised groups)
QUALIFICATIONS AND COURSES:	FEDAS, SSI
DISCOUNTS:	Groups and diving forfait
OTHER INFORMATION:	Transport service from the centre to the hotel

NAME OF CENTRE:	Escuba Palma
LOCATION:	Santa Ponça
ADDRESS:	Vía Rey Jaume I No.38
OPENING HOURS:	Departures at 10.00 and at 15.00 hours
TELEPHONE:	971 69 49 68 Fax: 971 69 20 84
LANGUAGES SPOKEN:	English, Spanish and German
BOAT:	Grand Banks 32 (11 metres) and a RIB
OTHER SERVICES:	Hire, retail and refill
ACCOMMODATION:	Hostal Oeste ***
CRUISES:	Yes
QUALIFICATIONS AND COURSES:	BASAC and CEMAS
ASSOCIATION:	British Sub Aqua Club
DISCOUNTS:	25% for groups or diving forfaits
OTHER INFORMATION:	Special dives

NAME OF CENTRE: CPIAS Nico Sport
LOCATION: Porto Cristo
MANAGER OR PROPRIETOR: Jaime Nicolau Rius
MANAGER'S QUALIFICATIONS: *** FEDAS, CMAS and Divemaster SSI
ADDRESS: Passeig cap des Toll, No.11
OPENING HOURS: 9.00 to 13.30 and from 16.00 to 20.00 hours
TELEPHONE: 971 82 27 39
LANGUAGES SPOKEN: Catalan, Spanish, English, German and French
BOAT: Gallart
OTHER SERVICES: Hiring of equipment and cylinder refilling
CRUISES: Own boat with a guide
QUALIFICATIONS AND COURSES: FEDAS, CMAS, SSI

NAME OF CENTRE: Centro de Formación de Instructores SSI
LOCATION: Baleares
MANAGER OR PROPRIETOR: Aníbal Alonso Homar
MANAGER'S QUALIFICATIONS: Instructor trainer
ADDRESS: C/ Magalhaes No 8. 07014 Palma
OPENING HOURS: 9.30 to 13.30 and 16.30 to 20.00
TELEPHONE: 971 73 09 43
LANGUAGES SPOKEN: Catalan, Spanish, English and French
BOAT: Yes
CRUISES: Own boat with guide
QUALIFICATIONS AND COURSES: Diving instructor courses
ASSOCIATION: SCUBA SCHOOLS INTERNATIONAL

NAME OF CENTRE: Club Actividades Subacuáticas TRITÓN
LOCATION: Palma
MANAGER OR PROPRIETOR: Club Social Tritón
MANAGER'S QUALIFICATIONS: Instructor ***
ADDRESS: C/ Roger de Llúria 4-A. 07014-Palma
OPENING HOURS: 19.00 to 21.30
TELEPHONE: 971 45 61 25
LANGUAGES SPOKEN: Catalan and Spanish
BOAT: 6 metre, 10 seat rigid inflatable boat
OTHER SERVICES: Social room, library, video library, speleo, medical
                          surgery, first aid, subaquatic photography
QUALIFICATIONS AND COURSES: All levels of FEDAS and SSI courses
ASSOCIATION: FEDAS and SSI

NAME OF CENTRE: Isurus Subaquatic
LOCATION: Palma de Mallorca
MANAGER OR PROPRIETOR: Aníbal Alonso Homar
MANAGER'S QUALIFICATIONS: Instructor trainer SSI, FEDAS instructor ***, N-4,
FEDAS-CMAS
ADDRESS: C/ Magalhaes No 8. 07014 Palma
OPENING HOURS: 9.30 to 13.30 and 16.30 to 20.00 hours
TELEPHONE: 971 73 09 43
LANGUAGES SPOKEN: Catalan, Spanish, English and French
BOAT: Motor yacht Princess 37
OTHER SERVICES: Retail, hire, repair, cylinder refill
ACCOMMODATION: It can be arranged
DISCOUNTS: For groups of more than 10
QUALIFICATIONS AND COURSES: SSI all levels
ASSOCIATION: SSI

NAME OF CENTRE: U.C.N.
LOCATION: Port Adriano. El Toro. Calvià
MANAGER OR PROPRIETOR: Antonio Iglesias Moral
MANAGER'S QUALIFICATIONS: Professional instructor, FEDAS, PADI
ADDRESS: Port Adriano s/n
OPENING HOURS: 9.30 to 13.30 and 16.00 to 20.00 hours
TELEPHONE: 971 10 26 76
LANGUAGES SPOKEN: Spanish, Catalan, English, German and French
BOAT: Three
OTHER SERVICES: Hyperbaric chamber, professional services, recognised
professional diving school
ACCOMMODATION: Various
QUALIFICATIONS AND COURSES: All associations
DISCOUNTS: 20% for pupils

NAME OF CENTRE: Octopus
LOCATION: Port de Sóller
MANAGER OR PROPRIETOR: Marc G. Chicano
MANAGER'S QUALIFICATIONS: PADI instructor
OPENING HOURS: 15th March to 30th October from 9.30 to 19.30 hours
TELEPHONE: 971 63 31 33 and 908 63 17 56
LANGUAGES SPOKEN: Spanish, Catalan, English, Italian and French
BOAT: 9 metres for 12 divers and a support 4 seat boat
OTHER SERVICES: Retail, hire, cylinder refill
ACCOMMODATION: Es Port Hotel and others
QUALIFICATIONS AND COURSES: PADI, specialities, FEDAS
DISCOUNTS: 8% at the hotel, and group discounts

NAME OF CENTRE:	Naviera Daedalus
LOCATION:	Port Adriano
MANAGER OR PROPRIETOR:	S.L.
MANAGER'S QUALIFICATIONS:	First class professional
DIVING SCHEDULE:	To be arranged
TELEPHONE:	989 68 23 72 and 971 61 62 26
LANGUAGES SPOKEN:	Spanish, Catalan, English and French
BOAT:	15 metre long Aresa
OTHER SERVICES:	Equipment to rent
ACCOMMODATION:	On the boat, between 6 and 8 people
DISCOUNTS:	5% for stays of more than one week

NAME OF CENTRE:	Scuba Pollentia
LOCATION:	Port de Pollença
MANAGER OR PROPRIETOR:	Matias Ximelis Roig
MANAGER'S QUALIFICATIONS:	Industrialist, diving instructor
ADDRESS:	C/ Vicente Buades, 28
OPENING HOURS:	8.30 to 20.00 hours
TELEPHONE:	971 86 79 78
LANGUAGES SPOKEN:	Spanish, Catalan, English, German and French
BOAT:	Gran Bank 32, 10 metres long, cap. 15 people.
OTHER SERVICES:	Cylinder refill
ACCOMMODATION:	Hostal, hotel or apartments
QUALIFICATIONS AND COURSES:	PADI, ACUC

ADDRESSES AND TELEPHONES
of interest for divers

ACCIDENT AND EMERGENCY 061

Federación Balear de Actividades Subacuáticas	971 46 33 15
IMI. La Casa del Mapa. Joan Maragall No.3 Palma	971 77 16 16
Seeman Sub España: wholesale of equipment	971 73 09 43
Escuela Náutica Palma	971 46 49 90
Naviera Daedalus Yacht Charter, diving cruises	971 61 62 26
Isurus, shop and instructor training SSI	971 73 09 43

Consell's fire brigade	971 17 35 52 and 085	Palma Airport	971 26 46 24
Palma fire brigade	971 29 12 50	Tourist information	902 20 22 02
Sóller fire brigade	971 63 25 00	Customs Vigilance Service	971 71 11 67
Sefobasa (forest brigade)	971 17 61 00	Naval Command	971 71 29 61 and 971 71 13 71
Icona:	971 71 17 77	Naval Sector (press)	971 71 03 49
Consellería Agricultura y Pesca	971 17 61 00	Taxis	908 53 80 81
Civil defense Autonomus Community	971 60 16 40	Army Geographic Service	91 711 50 43
Civil defense	971 21 81 00	Ambulance	061
National Insitute of Meteorology	971 40 36 00 and 971 40 35 11	MARITIME RESCUE	971 72 83 22
		Son Dureta Hospital	971 17 50 00
Police headquarters	971 28 08 00	Miramar Polyclinic	971 45 02 12
Civil Guard	971 46 51 12	Planas Clinic	971 73 88 43
Traffic Civil Guard	971 46 72 12	Juaneda Clinic	971 73 16 47
Palma Local Police	971 28 16 00	Red Cross Hospital	971 75 14 45 and 971 29 50 00
Grup Ornitología Balear	971 72 11 05	General Hospital	971 17 35 01
Greenpeace	971 40 58 12	Military Hospital	971 71 71 07
Air Rescue Services (SAR)	971 26 42 66 and 971 86 54 50	OTORHINOLARYNGOLOGIST	
Fishermen's guild	971 45 49 47	(diving specialist)	971 71 83 73
Port station	971 40 01 25		
Maritime safety	971 40 36 00	Hyperbaric chambers:	
Consumer's Association	971 71 70 78	Unidad Costa Norte	971 10 26 76
Port of Palma Civil guard	971 71 32 80	Hyperbaric chambers:	
Airport police station	971 26 46 59	Juaneda clinic	971 73 16 47 and
Equipment hire	971 28 71 69		908 53 45 54

CAULERPA TAXIFOLIA, THE "KILLER SEAWEED"

During the last few years it has been news in all the media. *Caulerpa taxifolia* or "killer seaweed" is a native plant of tropical waters, which is slowly taking root in the sandy bottom of Majorca's waters, and has put the public administrations on the rack because of its rapid expansion all over the Mediterranean sea floor.

The *Caulerpa* was detected for the first time in autumn 1991 along the French coast of Saint Cyprien, only 30 kilometres away from the Spanish frontier. Because it is a bentonic seawe-ed, *Caulerpa* establishes and thrives on the marine bottom according to its need for light, therefore it is limited to certain depths; in the western Mediterranean coasts it does not live beyond 80 metres of depth, and it also needs clear and clean waters. According to French scientific investigations, the killer seaweed established itself at the beginning of 1984 and it is believed that the first shoots came from the Monegasque Oceanographic Museum. In a short space of time it proliferated along the south coast of France,

Caulerpa taxifolia

extending various kilometres, maintaining its epicentre in the proximities of Saint Cyprien.

Caulerpa taxifolia has been for many years the favourite plant to adorn sea water aquariums with tropical species, which is why investigators believe that the first shoot "escaped" from the Monegasque Oceanographic Museum during a routine clean up of some thematic aquarium dedicated to the Caribbean seas.

The problem that the *Caulerpa* causes is its reproduction and invasion potential, which forces the Mediterranean native seaweeds out. It develops over practically any kind of substratum where hydrodynamics are not too violent and, although it prefers to establish between 0 and 35 metres of depth, it is unknown whether or not it has reached lower depths which are harder to access for divers.

As it forces the native seaweeds out, it causes an impoverishment of the marine fauna because up until now, the organisms that feed from the native seaweeds of the Mediterranean cannot substitute them for the *Caulerpa* because of its high content in specific toxins. In its natural habitat it has predators, but there are no fish in the Balearic sea that can biologically control it, so its expansion is limited only by its light needs, the depth, and its capacity to advance.

How this killer seaweed reached the Balearic coasts is not known exactly; it has been speculated that a shoot from the south of France arrived on one of the many leisure yachts that visit Majorca during the summer, caught onto the anchor. It has also been thought that it could have arrived pushed by the strong currents of the León gulf. It does not matter how it happened.... the thing is, it is here.

There are still many unanswered questions about the *Caulerpa*; we do not know its origin, its degree of expansion, nor its real incidence over the native life of the Mediterranean waters; what we do know is that we can and must inform the competent authorities when we see it in the Balearic sea, so that the experts can decide what to do.

MOST COMMON SPECIES IN THE BALEARIC SEA

ABALONE: *Haliotis tuberculata*, oreja de mar, orella de mar, ormeau, Seeohr.

AMBER JACK: *Seriola dumerili*, serviola, serviola, sériole, Seriolafisch.

ANGLERFISH: *Lophius piscatorius*, rape, rap, baudroie, Seeteufel.

ANNULAR BREAM: *Diplodus annularis*, raspallón, esparrall, sparaillon, Ringelbrasse.

AXILLARY WRASSE: *Symphodus mediterraneus*, vaqueta, canari, crénilabre rouquié.

BARRACUDA: *Sphyraena sphyraena*, espetón, espet, brochet de mer, Pfeilhecht.

BASS: *Dicentrarchus labrax*, lubina, llobarro, lobine, Wolfsbarsch.

BEADLET ANEMONE: *Actinia equina*, tomate de mar, ortiga roja, actinie rouge, Erdbeerseerose.

BLONDE RAY: *Raja brachyura*, raya común, rajada, raie lisse, Zitterfisch.

BLUE SHARK: *Prionace glauca*, tintorera, tintorera, requin bleu, Blauhai.

BLUEFIN TUNE: *Thunnus Thynnus*, atun rojo, tonyina, thon rouge, Roter Thun.

BOGUE: *Boops boops*, boga, boga, bogue, Gelbstriemen.

BROWN MEAGRE: *Sciaena umbra*, corvallo, corball, corbeau, Seebarbe.

BROWN WRASSE: *Labrus merula*, merlo, tord massot, merle, brauner Lippfisch.

CAPE TOWN LOBSTER: *Scyllarides latus*, cigarra de mar, cigala, grande cigale, grosser Bärenkrebs.

CARDINALFISH: *Apogon imberbis*, reyezuelo, reietó, roi des rougets, Meerbarbenkönig.

CLEAVER WRASSE: *Xyrichtis novacula*, Galán, raó, rason.

COMB GROUPET: *Mycteroperca rubra*, gitano, anfós rosat, mérou royal.

COMBER: *Serranus cabrilla*, cabrilla, serrà, serran petite chèvre, Blutstriemen.

COMMON CUTTLEFISH: *Sepia officinalis*, sepia, sípia, seiche commune, gemeiner Tintenfisch.

COMMON LOBSTER: *Homarus gammarus*, bogavante, grimald, homard, Hummer.

COMMON OCTOPUS: *Octopus vulgaris*, pulpo, pop roquer, pieuvre, Krake.

COMMON SOLE: *Solea solea*, lenguado, llenguado, sole commune, Seezunge.

COMMON STING-RAY: *Dasyatis pastinaca*, chucho, escorçó, pastenague, Stechrochen.

CONGER EEL: *Conger conger*, congrio, congre, congre, Meeraal.

CRAB: *Calappa granulata*, cangrejo real, cranc rei, crabe honteux, Schamkrabbe.

CRAB: *Eriphia spinifrons*, cangrejo peludo, cranc pelut, crabe jaune, Krabbe.

CRIMPY JELLYFISH: *Cotylorhiza tuberculata*, aguacajada, acalef cresp, acalèphe crepé, Qualle.

DAMSELFISH: *Chromis chromis*, castañuela, tuta, castagnole, Mönchsfisch.

DENTEX: *Dentex dentex*, denton, déntol, denté, Zahnbrasse.

EUROPEAN SQUID: *Loligo vulgaris*, calamar, calamar, calmar, Kalmar.

FALSE CORAL: *Myriapora truncata*, falso coral, corall bord, faux corail.

FALSE CORAL: *Parerythropodium coralloides*, falso coral, fals corall, faux corail, Trugkoralle.

FAN MUSSEL CRAB: *Pinnotheres pinnotheres*, cangrejo de la nacra, cranc de nacra.

FAN MUSSEL: *Pinna nobilis*, nacra, nacra, nacre, Steckmuschel.

FLATHEAD GREY MULLET: *Mugil cephalus*, lisa, llissa llobarrera, Mulet a grosse tête.

FLYING GURNARD: *Cephalacantus volitans*, chicharra, xoric, grodin volant, Flughahn.

GARFISH: *Belone belone*, aguja, agulla, orphie, Hornhecht

GILTHEAD: *Sparus auratus*, dorada, orada, dorade, Goldbrassen

GOLDEN GROUPER: *Epinephelus alexandrinus*, falso abadejo, anfós llis, badèche.

GOOSEMECK BARNACLE: *Lepas anatifera*, anatifa, anatifa, anatife, Entenmuschel.

GREAT HERMIT CRAB: *Dardanus arrosor*, ermitaño, ermità gros, bernard ermite, grosser Einsiedler-krebs.

GREATER FORKBEARD: *Phycis phycis*, brótola, mòllera, moustelle brune, Mittelmeertrüsche.

GREATER WEEVER: *Trachinus draco*, araña, aranya blanca, grande vive, Petermännchen.

GREEN WRASSE: *Labrus viridis*, grivia, tord, labre vert, grüner Lippfisch.

GROUPER: *Epinephelus guaza*, mero, anfós, mérou, großer Sägebarsch.

JELLYFISH: *Rhizostoma pulmo*, aguamala, borm blau, rhizostome, Wurzelmundqualle.

JOHN DORY: *Zeus faber*, pez San Pedro, gall, saint pierre, Petersfisch.

LARGE SCALED SCORPION FISH: *Scorpaena scrofa*, cabracho, cap-roig, rascasse rouge, großer Drachenkopf.

LESSER OCTOPUS: *Eledone cirrhosa*, pulpo blanco, pop trobiguera, poulpe blanc, kleine Krake.

LITTLE CUTTLEFISH: *Sepia elegans*, chopito, sípia de punxa, petite seiche, kleine Sepia.

LONG SPINED SEA URCHIN: *Centrostephanus longispinus*, puercoespín marino, eriçó de punxes llargues, oursin rouge à longs piquants, langstachliger Seeigel.

MACKEREL SHARK: *Isurus oxyrinchus*, marrajo, tauró, taupe bleue, Heringshai.

MARBLED ELECTRIC RAY: *Torpedo marmorata*, tremielga, vaca tremolosa, torpille marbrée, marmorierter Zitterroche.

MERMAID'S VEIL: *Setella cellulosa*, encaje, encaix, voile de neptune, Neptunschleier.

MORAY EEL: *Muraena helena*, morena, morena, murène, Muräne.

MULTICOLOURED VIOLESCENT SEA-WHIP: *Aparamunicea chamaleon*, gorgonia violácea, gorgònia, gorgone, violette Gorgonie.

OCRE HACKLED STARFISH: *Astropecten aurantiacus*, estrella anaranjada de arena, estrella, astérie dentelée, roter Kammstern.

ORNATE WRASSE: *Thalassoma pavo*, fredi, fadrí, girelle paon, Meerplaw.

PAINTED COMBER: *Serranus scriba*, serrano, vaca, serran écriture, Schriftbarsch.

PEACOCK WRASSE: *Symphodus tinca*, peto, tord, crénilabre tanche, Pfauenlippfisch.

PELTODORIS: *Peltodoris atromaculata*, vaquita suiza, vaqueta suïssa, doris maculé.

PILOTFISH: *Naucrates ductor*, pez piloto, pàmpol, poisson pilote, Lotsenfisch.

PINK JELLYFISH: *Pelagia noctiluca*, medusa, medusa luminiscent, acalèphe brillante, Leuchtqualle.

PLAIN BONITO: *Auxis thazard*, mélvera, melva, bonitou, unechter Bonito.

POSIDONIA: *Posidonia oceanica*, posidonia, posidònia, alga, paille de mer, Neptungras.

PRAWN: *Palaemon elegans*, quisquilla, gambeta, bouquet, Garneele.

RAINBOW WRASSE: *Thalassoma pavo*, galán, fadrí, girelle paon, Meerplaw.

RAINBOW: *Coris julis*, doncella, donzella, girelle, Meerjunker.

RED BANDFISH: *Cepola macrophthalma*, cinta, veta, cépole, roter Bandfisch.

RED MULLET: *Mullus barbatus*, salmonete de fango, moll de fang, rouget barbet, rote Meerbarbe.

RED STARFISH: *Echinaster sepositus*, estrella, estrella vermella, étoile de mer rouge, roter Seestern.

ROCK BLENNY: *Parablennius gattorugine*, cabruza, bavosa, baveuse, gestreifter Schleimfisch.

SADDLED BREAM: *Oblada melanura*, oblada, oblada, blade, Brandbrasse.

SARDINIE CORAL: *Corallium rubrum*, coral rojo, corall vermell, corail rouge, Edelkoralle.

SAUPE: *Sarpa salpa*, salpa, salpa, saupe, Goldstrieme.

SCORPIONFISH: *Scorpaena porcus*, rascacio, escórpora, rascasse brune, brauner Drachenkopf.

SEA HORSE: *Hyppocampus hyppocampus*, caballito de mar, cavall marí, cheval marin, Seepferdchen.

SEASUCKER: *Aplisia depilans*, liebre de mar, llebre de mar, lièvre de mer, gefleckter Seehase.

SHORT SUNFISH: *Mola mola*, pez luna, lluna, poisson-lune, Mondfisch.

SMALL RED SCORPION FISH: *Scorpaena notata*, escórpora de fango, catpinyós, petite rascasse.

SNAKELOCKS ANEMONE: *Anemonia sulcata*, anémona, fideu, anémone de mer, Wachsrose.

SPINY LOBSTER: *Palinurus vulgaris*, langosta, llagosta, langouste, Languste.

SPOTTED WEEVER: *Trachinus radiatus*, araña negra, aranya de cap negre, vive rayée, Mittelländische Queise.

STREAKED GURNARD: *Trigloporus lastoviza*, rubio, gallineta, grondin strié, gestreifter Seehahn.

STRIPED RED MULLET: *Mullus surmuletus*, salmonete de roca, moll roquer, rouget de roche, gestreifte Meerbarbe.

STRIPED GREY MULLET: *Mugil cephalus*, mújol, llissa, mulet à grosse tête, grossköpfige Meerasche.

SWALLOWTAIL SEA PERCH: *Anthias anthias*, tres colas, dentó, barbier, Rötling.

SWORDFISH: *Xiphias gladius*, pez espada, emperador, espadón, Schwertfisch.

TRIGGERFISH: *Balistes carolinensis*, pez ballesta, surer, baliste, Druckerfisch.

TWO-BANDED BREAM: *Diplodus vulgaris*, mojarra, variada, sargue, gewöhnliche Geissbrasse.

WHITE BREAM: *Diplodus sargus*, sargo, sarg, sar, grosser Geissbrasse.

WIDE-EYED FLOUNDER: *Bothus podas*, pez plano, pedaç, platophrys, augenfleckiger Steinbutt.

WREATHY-TUFT: *Spirographis spallanzanii*, espirógrafo, cuc de flor, espirographe, Schraubensabelle.

YELLOW SEA-WHIP: *Eunicella verrucosa*, gorgonia blanca, gorgònia blanca, gorgone jaune, gelbe Gorgonie.

TELECOMMUNICATIONS AT SEA

In Region 1, where Spain is, the assigned frequencies to the mobile maritime service stations that function in the frequency bands between 1.905 and 3.800 KHz must be chosen within the following bands whenever possible:

1.605 - 1.625 KHz	Radiotelegraphy only.
1.625 - 1.670 KHz	low power.
1.670 - 1.950 KHz	coastal stations.
1.950 - 2.053 KHz	from boat station to coast station.
2.053 - 2.170 KHz	communications between boats.
2.173,5 - 2.190,5 KHz	SOS GUARD BAND AND 2.182 KHz CALLS
2.194 - 2.440 KHz	communications between boats
2.578 - 2.850 KHz	coastal stations
3.340 - 3.600 KHz	communications between boats

INTERNATIONAL RADIO CODE FOR SPELLED CALLS

A	alfa	N	november
B	bravo	O	oscar
C	charlie	P	papa
D	delta	Q	quebec
E	echo	R	romeo
F	foxtrot	S	sierra
G	golf	T	tango
H	hotel	U	uniform
I	india	V	victor
J	juliett	W	whiskey
K	kilo	X	x-ray
L	lima	Y	yankee
M	mike	Z	zulu

IT IS FORBIDDEN

To make unnecessary transmissions.

To make unidentified or false signals.

To make transmissions to an officially NOT recognised station.

To transmit inside the port within the frequency margins of 1.670 KHz to 2.850 KHz, except for justified SOS, emergency and safety cases.

MARITIME LEGISLATION

RESCUE, FINDS AND EXTRACTIONS

The law 60/1962 of 24th December 1962, regulates the maritime help, rescue, tugging, findings and extractions.

CHAPTER I. Help and rescue

Article One: the help and rescue of maritime navigation ships or aeroplanes at sea that are in a danger situation, the equipment on board, the charter and transportation charges, as well as the services of the same kind that the ships give to each other, are submitted to the following rules, regardless of the waters in which the services have been given.

Article Two: any help or rescue action that produces a beneficial outcome will result in a fair remuneration. There will be no remuneration if the action does not have a beneficial outcome. The total amount due to pay can never exceed the value of the rescued things. The remuneration requested as a consequence of a rescue action will be paid by the rescued ship owner or the salvaged aeroplane's operator.

Article Three: those who take part in any rescue operation in spite of an express and reasonable prohibition by the aided ships, will not be entitled to any reward.

Article Four: the rescue operations between ships that navigate or fish as a unit are not entitled to a reward, unless they are done in exceptional conditions of difficulty and risk.

Article Six: the parties involved in the rescue will agree the right amount for the reward, failing that, the Central Maritime Court will decide.

Article Eight: any assistance agreement stipulated under the influence of the danger can be modified by request of one of the parts by the Central Maritime Court.

Article Ten: the people who have been rescued are not required to pay any compensation.

Article Eleven: the legal action for the payment of the compensation prescribes after two years from the day in which the rescue operations ceased.

CHAPTER III.
Findings at sea

Article Nineteen: whoever finds abandoned things at sea must put them at the disposition of the Marine Authorities as soon as possible. Whoever extracts sunken items has the same obligation, and must do it immediately after having discovered them.

Article Twenty: the things that have been found will be returned to their owner if he appears and proves ownership, having to pay first the expenses and a third of the items' value.

Article Twenty-one: if after the appointed six months the owner does not appear and the value of the items does not exceed 150 thousand pesetas, they will be given to the finder, after he pays for the expenses. If the value exceeds 150 thousand pesetas, the finder will be entitled to that amount plus one third of the excess obtained at the public auction. This chapter is not applicable to abandoned ships.

CHAPTER IV. Extractions

Article Twenty-three: out of the cases of findings and of immediate recoveries, the extraction of sunken goods in Spanish jurisdictional waters requires the permission of the Marine Authority.

Article Twenty-four: the works of exploration, search and location of sunken goods require prior permission from the MA, who will grant it at its discretion and without exclusivity.

Article Twenty-five: the extraction of sunken goods within the ports will be determined by the ports legislation.

Article Twenty-seven: When the sunken goods do not constitute any danger for navigation, the Marine Authorities will allow the owners to proceed with their extraction.

Article Twenty-eight: in the cases in which the ownership belongs to the State and the extraction is not convenient, the Marine Ministry can grant the extraction and exploitation of the goods by public auction.

CHAPTER V. The property rights of the found effects.

Article Twenty-nine: the State will acquire the property right of any sunken ship or object, salvaged or found when its owner has abandoned his rights or fails to practice them within the following periods.

A) ships or remains of ships, three years after they were sunk.

B) all other cases, six months after publication of the edict.

These periods will be interrupted when the extraction is requested and started within the period granted for it.

Article Thirty: the Marine Authority, to avoid the loss or destruction of ships or found goods, can decide to sell them in a public auction before the periods of property prescribe, placing the corresponding part of the obtained value of them at the disposition of their owner until he appears or the right extinguishes.

TRANSPORTS

THE MINISTRY OF TRANSPORT, TOURISM AND COMMUNICATIONS STIPULATES:

Article 1: There is an established zone in the sea along the coastline, of 200 metres in width for the beaches and 50 metres for the rest of the coastline, where, when bathers or swimmers use it, it is forbidden to practice any sports or leisure activity that uses a boat or any device with a propeller, or that without a propeller can reach speeds of over three knots.

Article 3: At the beaches, coves, etc. where there are bathers and where any nautical sport is practised with crafts with a propeller or a sail that reach more than three knots of speed, the local Marine Authority will determine starting, mooring or beaching channels for such crafts, which will have to be correctly indicated and within which swimming is forbidden.

Article 6: Sports crafts inside the ports and their access channels will avoid interference with the normal traffic of the port, and in no case must they prompt the ships navigating to manoeuvre.

ANNEX: those who perform dives without air cylinders will indicate their position with a red spherical buoy with a white band, and those who dive with cylinders will visibly carry on their boat an A (ALFA) flag of the International Flag Code. The boats will give these marks a minimum sea room of 25 metres.

MADRID, 2nd JULY 1964